Money Minder
Simplify, Organize and Manage Your Personal Financial Records

Michal E. Feder

LIBERTY HOUSE®

Second Edition • First Printing

Library of Congress Cataloging in Publication Data

Feder, Michal E.
   Money minder.

   1. Finance, Personal. 2. Records—Management.
I. Title.
HG179.F38   1989   332.024   88-13818
ISBN 0-8306-3039-2 (pbk.)

TAB BOOKS Inc. offers software for sale. For information and a catalog, please contact TAB Software Department, Blue Ridge Summit, PA 17294-0850.

Questions regarding the content of this book should be addressed to:

Reader Inquiry Branch
TAB BOOKS Inc.
Blue Ridge Summit, PA 17294-0214

This publication is dedicated to anyone who, like myself, has ever struggled to master the art of managing financial records.

My thanks to the many people who have been interested and encouraging. I would like to particularly acknowledge those who gave generously of their time, expertise, and advice. Special thanks to Financial Advisors Sandra Pazahin and Phil Stelling; MONEY MINDER Pioneers, Bev Cone, Sue Kollmar, and Leslie Ann Williams; Editorial Advisors, Betty Bullock, Rick Ellwood, Joe Foust, Walter Moeller, Fran Tompakov, Mary Ann Weisberg, and Martin L. Ernst.

Edited by Eileen P. Baylus

►*Contents*

Ready Reference

►*INTRODUCTION*

INTRODUCTION

Welcome to the world of **MONEY MINDER**. The word *money* is loaded with mixed meanings and feelings about responsibility, tedious record-keeping, and the like. I created **MONEY MINDER** because I enjoy having and spending money a lot more than I like keeping track of it.

When I started to be serious about keeping track, I found the forms already available had been developed with an ''accountant'' mentality—that is, by people who like data and can write neatly and consistently, using forms with small columns and lots of figures on one sheet. In contrast, my normal handwriting is large, I make lots of mistakes in working with numbers, and pages covered with data automatically depress me.

So, I designed my own system with five criteria in mind:

Simplicity—the simplest form that would provide the information needed
Clarity—easy to read, easy to understand
Time—the minimum number of repeated actions
Accuracy—the fewest possible transfers of numbers (less chance for mistakes)
Pay-off—the most useful, accessible records maintained with the least amount of effort.

I started by studying other forms and removing everything I did not consider essential. It has taken me about five years of experimenting to develop the format you will be trying, and *it is still evolving*.

Each **MONEY MINDER** form creates a framework. Most of them are pretty straightforward. The *sample sheets* will show you how they *might* look when used. You probably will not want or need to use all of them. *Do not be afraid to skip all over the place and play with the forms in any order you choose.*

As you explore, think how you might customize your master forms so when you reprint them they fit your needs even better: For example, a friend suggested that I add the stock exchange symbol and certificate number to my stock form because she holds stock in her own name. Since I do not, I left it off my form but left space so you can add it to your master.

MONEY MINDER does not attempt to guide you in investment choices. There are many professionals, books, courses, and personal mentors who can help you make good choices. The forms simplify and clarify the process of tracking money. By doing a better job of record-keeping, you will save *time* and *frustration*, and always *know where you are* . As a result, it will be easier for you to make wise investment decisions when an opportunity comes along.

MONEY MINDER is a reference tool for creating your *own* simple system. To do that you will need a three-ring binder—preferably 1"—with pockets on the inside covers, front, and back. Pick a color you like. Nothing dreary.

MONEY MINDER folds open so you can duplicate forms easily. Keep it intact. Put copies of the forms into your notebook *as you start to use them.*

At first you might be overwhelmed by the number of forms in **MONEY MINDER**. Many of them will not apply to your situation. Others need only be filled out once a year or quarterly. For some, such as **HOME** or **PERSONAL PROPERTY**, you might add two or three lines a year once you have spent ten to fifteen minutes setting them up.

Anacaria Myrrha and Laurel Jensen, organization specialists, stress the importance of the right *label*, the right *location*, and the right *process* in helping their clients to set up effective files and manage their desktops. There is a natural parallel for managing your financial records.

Using the **MONEY MINDER** system, the right *label* involves choosing the right form to use. The right *location* means key information on your forms in your notebook and the backup or reference data in files, nearby, in storage, or in the wastebasket. The right *process* you must provide. That means pick the forms that will produce the records you want or need. Update them at the right time when you are handling the statement or report. Like a well managed filing system, money-minding does involve a few decisions; but once started, maintenance is not time-consuming and the psychic as well as actual energy saved is enormous.

To help in selecting the right forms, I've included several formats.

RECIPE FOR RECORDS shows you the easiest way to start getting your records under control. p. 11

CLEARING OUT THE CLUTTER has you select the area that is causing the most grief or needs immediate attention. p. 13

QUESTIONS, QUESTIONS, QUESTIONS points you to the forms that will organize different parts of your financial information for specific purposes. p. 14

Remember: Keep the forms in this book as *masters*. Make copies to work with in developing your own **MONEY MINDER** Notebook.

Tips:

- ☐ Use ink for any entry you are sure of.
- ☐ Use an erasable pen or pencil for the others. (I make so many mistakes I always use erasable pens because it bothers me to mess up a form.)
- ☐ When in doubt, make an educated guess—in erasable pen or pencil.
- ☐ Code by color. Example: Blue = High Priority, Brown = Necessity, Green = Hopes and Dreams, Red = Special/Personal. (Pick colors that have meaning for you.)
- ☐ Use the "Prepared _____" space in the upper left corner of the forms to date when you record information. It will become increasingly valuable over time when you refer back to a form for information or to update it.

Start right away to become more efficient about how you handle financial information coming to you. When you first look it over, highlight the key information for quick referral in the future. About 80 to 90 percent of most forms you deal with is support information or technical details. Because each form is different, it pays to learn the layout of yours and save time and energy whenever you refer back.

Here's an example:

1

Money Fund

Year to Date
Confirmation Statement
SEE REVERSE SIDE FOR INFORMATION ABOUT YOUR STATEMENT

ACCOUNT NUMBER	SOCIAL SECURITY OR TAXPAYER IDENTIFICATION NO	REPRESENTATIVE	SPONSOR NUMBER
1013322	123-45-6789 INVESTOR	SPONSOR	77777000

IDA SMART
101 MEMORY LANE
BIG CITY, CA 94104

NO DEALER OF RECORD

SUMMARY OF YOUR ACCOUNT

STATEMENT DATE	INCOME DIVIDENDS PAID THIS YEAR	CAPITAL GAINS PAID THIS YEAR	CERTIFICATE SHARES HELD BY YOU	+	SHARES HELD BY THE BANK	=	TOTAL SHARES YOU OWN
04/13/88	$35.12	$0.00	0.000		2,278.251		2,278.251
DISTRIBUTIONS REINV							

Managing Yourself

It's easy these days to find a wealth of material on how to manage your money, how to time your investments, how to diversify and handle risk. Very little is written about what I have found to be the critical first step—managing yourself. About 12 years ago, I happened upon a book called *How To Get Rich Slowly But Almost $urely* by William T. Morris. One paragraph struck a nerve and I have found myself living out its truth ever since.

"The thing which most distinguishes the amateur from the professional in financial operations is, simply self awareness. The secret of the professional, I'm now convinced, is the discovery that they can dramatically increase their chances of success by watching themselves even more carefully than they watch the market. The thing about the pros is not so much the specific knowledge of investment opportunities they have, but the fact that they know enough about themselves to protect themselves from themselves."

What is it you need to know about yourself and pay attention to even more closely than changes, opportunities, and developments in the world of money? Here's a simple exercise that might help get you started in asking yourself the right questions.

Put an x along the dotted lines for how you see yourself as a *money manager* today. Do it in pencil because you might be in for some surprises. As you think about yourself and watch yourself in action, you will find there is a pattern to your behavior. As an investor *and* a records manager, I have found it is important to know yourself and protect yourself from your foibles.

Saver . . . . Spender
(Always pay yourself first)   (Never manage to have any left
                                                   over)

Dependent . . . . Independent
(Like advice, help, direction in   (Need to know, understand, willing
making money decisions. Want to   to take responsibility, credit for
rely on the experts)   choices)

Careful . . . . Intuitive
(Want lots of information before   (Might research but rely on gut
deciding)   feelings)

Risk avoider . . . . Risk taker
(Like to stick with known   (Willing to take chances on
results/probably lower rewards)   possibilities & chance of high
                                                   rewards)

Organized . . . . Disorganized
(Keep your financial & personal   (Keep stuff in files, drawers &
papers in order and up-to-date)   & closets. No consistency or order
                                                   in papers or procedures)

Neat . . . . Messy
(Clear handwriting, keep notes)   (Sloppy or large handwriting, few
                                                   notes and often can't read or
                                                   remember what you wrote)

For example, I have almost no resistance to possibilities. Every time I read about an interesting stock I want to buy it. To manage myself, because I also want some degree of known results, I invest almost entirely in mutual funds and limit my risk taking to aggressive funds.

Because I like possibilities, I tend to accumulate too much information and advice before acting. Delaying decisions has cost me far more over the years than the choices I have actually made. To handle this tendency, I resist/limit my exposure to suggestions, prospectuses, workshops, and advisors. I use them very selectively and consciously.

My biggest issue was my personal financial records. To manage the controlled chaos I had created for myself, I decided to give up guilt for gain and design a records management system to save or make me money. I based it on the premise that a simple form completed and kept current was a lot better than none at all. Fifteen years later I am absolutely convinced that I am much richer than I would have been otherwise.

The unexpected and wholly delightful result of this research in self-awareness and self-management is a sense of mastery that is hard to describe but wonderful to experience. The bad news is that you have to act to get there. The good news is that it is not nearly as hard or as time-consuming as you think.

Start to do a better job of managing your records by examining your attitudes or what I call getting to "start." It's like getting ready for a race or starting a business project. Some preparation has to occur beforehand. So spend a bit of time thinking positively about what pay off you might get from doing a better job. More money? Less guilt? Less wasted time? More organized? A greater sense of control? More self-esteem? If you can identify two or three good reasons to change or improve your records it will help you get started.

Secondly, be realistic about the time and energy you are willing to devote to your records. You are already doing something with every minute of the day. Take a look at your life and pick a reasonable amount of time, preferably at a time of day when you typically have a lot of energy. Starting and failing is depressing. *Don't start until you are ready to schedule time on a regular basis.* Most records-aversive types will need to think of these sessions as appointments and treat them that way. That is, don't break them except in an emergency.

Forget about answers such as when and how to and concentrate on the questions. Ask yourself:

What's not working now?_____

_____

What would you like your records to accomplish?

_____

What records are incomplete that now cost you time, money, aggravation?_____

_____

What records could *save* you time, money, aggravation?

_____

The clearer you are about what kind of person you are, what you want for yourself and what you are ready to do about it, the more likely you are to act in ways that will make it happen. In fact, until the vision is pretty clear in your own mind, very little is likely to change.

Records Management

When I started to get serious about improving my own financial record system, I decided to approach it not as a well-known enemy, but just another business problem. I quickly discovered that in addition to all the emotional baggage and a general distaste for numbers, there was a good deal of confusion in how I thought about records. The same was true for most of the people I talked to. None of us had spent much time viewing the subject objectively.

The first step in taking a fresh approach involved unraveling what Dr. Theodore Rubin calls muddles. These are words that are similar but have significant differences. Here are some muddles that need to be understood in thinking about records:

Collect vs Organize: Many people believe that collecting information and keeping it sorted in neat piles or files is organizing it. The significant element that is lost is that of purpose or unity. To be organized is to arrange thoughtfully with a concern for interdependence and coherence.

Keep vs Manage: Keeping records is certainly the first step in managing them but managing, as a quick trip to your dictionary will confirm, includes the notion of control and care and the act of altering and manipulating.

Structure vs System: Combining various elements in an organized way creates a structure or framework for your financial information. It is the methods and procedures that you use in interacting with the structure that turn it into a system.

Freedom vs Responsibility: Many people see these words as opposites. To them freedom is being able to turn money matters over to the experts or to be free to ignore bank statements and other financial information. They would define responsibility as accountability and a burden.

I would argue that, as the dictionary defines it, responsibility is first and foremost the ability to respond and that having that ability and being able to use it gives you far greater freedom than dependency on others. No matter how well intentioned and able your financial advisors are, you are ultimately accountable for documents you sign or actions that are executed on your behalf. Except in rare cases, you are bound by (not free of) the decisions and actions they take as your representative. So, the best way out of this muddle is to be sufficiently responsible to be able to hold your financial advisors accountable.

This system is based on the following beliefs:

- ☐ Effective records are the cornerstone of any sound system of money management.
- ☐ Systems are easier than any other way. Consistency saves time and energy.
- ☐ All records are not the same.
- ☐ All parts of any record or piece of financial information are not equally important and should not be treated as if they were.
- ☐ Record-keeping does not have to be boring.
- ☐ Gain is a better motivator than guilt. The stronger and more positive the motivation the more likely the follow through.

MONEY MINDER was designed with those beliefs in mind. A simple way to reframe how you think about records is to notice that there are three main categories of financial information and three basic things you can do with it.

BASELINE is the word I use for financial information that is permanent or semipermanent. Your date and place of birth never change so all you want is the correct record in an accessible place on the few occasions you need it. Semipermanent records might need tracking or evaluating occasionally.

MAINTENANCE is the word I chose to describe the information about money flowing in and out of your life that is periodic, changing, and primarily related to maintaining yourself. You can record, track, and evaluate it.

INVESTMENT describes the extra money in your life and what you do with it. All three ways of dealing with this information can be important to you.

Kinds of Information	*What you can do with it*		
	Record . . . . (collect)	**Track** . . . . (follow)	**Evaluate** . . . . (judge)
Baseline			
(Permanent or Semipermanent)			
Home	*Deed* *Title Insurance*	*Taxes* *changes in*	*Appraisals*
Will	*the document*	*federal law*	*Review it*
Trusts	*the document*	*Update it*	
Property			
Advisors			
Personal			

Maintenance
(current, changing)

Income . . . .

Expenses(Personal) . . . .

Expenses(Business) . . . .

Investment
(growth, future oriented)
Savings, interest, income oriented . . . .

Equity (ownership growth oriented) . . . .

☐ *Systematic record keeping* keeps you out of trouble, saves you time and aggravation and provides some sense of control.

☐ *Tracking* makes it possible to spot trends, make knowledgeable adjustments and reasonable projections.

☐ *Evaluating* helps you avoid past mistakes, identify realistic choices, make better decisions (based more on reality and less on emotion), and experience being in charge.

Finally, the importance of high-quality information cannot be overemphasized. You can set up a wonderful system and conscientiously go through all the steps of maintaining it and accomplish very little if the information you record and work with isn't

☐ **Accurate** (correct)
☐ **Adequate** (sufficient, complete)
☐ **Timely** (available when needed)
☐ **Reliable** (can be counted on)

You might not always be able to control the sources of your financial information, but it helps tremendously to be aware of the pitfalls of allowing a breakdown in the quality of your information.

Here are some examples:

Not accurate:

Stock certificates received from an inheritance were not identified as coming from two different trusts. Being told that signing an insurance application was only preliminary and would not become effective until passing a medical exam. The bank started charging my account immediately.

Not adequate:

Car insurance quote did not include the information that it was a preliminary price and could be increased after six months. Nothing was said about cancellation policy (my current policy can never be cancelled—a valuable element). The administrator of my Retirement Plan sent a notice (Form 5498) that says I made a "Rollover IRA contribution" in 1987. What it means is they are classifying it as a "purchase rollover," which means to them a transfer not a purchase!

Not timely:

Information regarding two limited partnerships arrived following the April 15 deadline forcing me to file for an extension and hope that I had paid enough to avoid a penalty. What this means for many of us is that we overpay and the government gets to use our money free in the meantime.

Not reliable:

Prices per share were given for inherited stocks that did not take into account stock splits during the past year. Number of shares inherited from two sources turned out seven months later to be incorrect. So was the cost basis. The IRS regularly supplies information on the phone but refuses to guarantee its reliability.

The most pernicious of these four criteria is adequate. It is very hard sometimes to know what you don't know so you can ask the right questions. It pays to keep saying, "What else do I need to know?"

Recipe for Records*

Ingredients: 1/2 hour spent reviewing **MONEY MINDER**
The forms in **MONEY MINDER**
Photocopies of the forms you want to try
An erasable pen
A highlighter
A generous amount of healthy optimism

Process: Start filling in any form. Date it.

Spend 15 to 30 minutes.

Put whatever you've accomplished into your new **MONEY MINDER** notebook.

Throw away any papers you have used that do not need to be saved. File the rest, highlighting key information you might want to refer to in the future.

Congratulate yourself and go off and celebrate.

Repeat this process once a week. First update the forms you already have in your notebook. Then work on adding in new ones.

Close the door on the past. Do not waste time going back and recapturing history *unless you have a specific present need*. (Examples: You are selling a stock or fund and need to verify all of the distributions you have reinvested to establish an accurate cost basis. Or you are selling your home and want to verify and summarize capital improvements.)

---

*Used with consistency and a reasonable degree of care, this recipe will support and satisfy you for a lifetime!

Clearing Out the Clutter

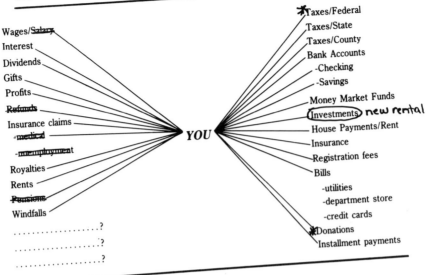

MONEY IN

MONEY OUT

Wages/~~Salary~~
Interest
Dividends
Gifts
Profits
~~Refunds~~
Insurance claims
~~-medical~~
~~-unemployment~~
Royalties
Rents
~~Pensions~~
Windfalls

. . . . ?
. . . . ?
. . . . ?

YOU

Taxes/Federal
Taxes/State
Taxes/County
Bank Accounts
-Checking
-Savings
Money Market Funds
(Investments) new rental
House Payments/Rent
Insurance
Registration fees
Bills
-utilities
-department store
-credit cards
Donations
Installment payments

1. Cross out every item in both columns that are *not* part of your life today.
2. Study the list and * the ones that bother you most.
3. Circle the items that have tax consequences and for which you do not have a satisfactory record-keeping process.

ACTION STEPS:

continue to consolidate tax records
Develop a new form for rental property
Make a master list of regular donations
(include last year's date and amount)

When people talk about the ways they get bogged down in their records, often one or two trouble spots account for most of the misery. I have used this exercise in workshops to help identify the specific set of records that needs immediate attention and also the ones that will bring the greatest psychological relief. I think it's important to handle those first. Small successes might spur you on to further efforts.

CLEARING OUT THE CLUTTER asks you to deal first with trouble in the present, then with the future, and then write down the steps you, or anyone you can recruit, must take to clear it up. It might be a one time problem like an insurance claim or an ongoing one for which one of the **MONEY MINDER** forms can help. The clutter is probably not just on your desk but in your mind. Do yourself a favor and limit yourself to moving ahead one step at a time.

Clearing Out the Clutter

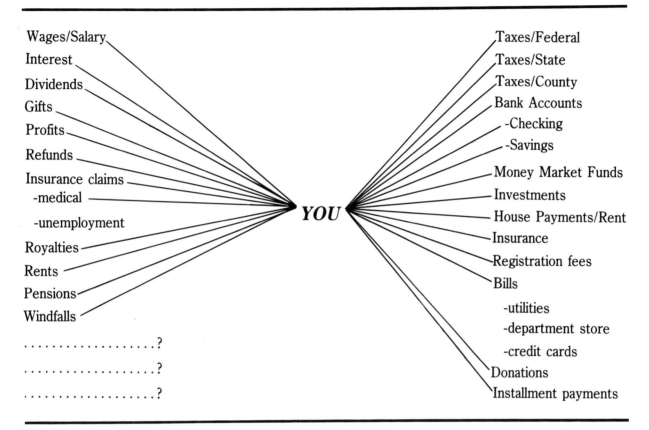

MONEY IN

Wages/Salary
Interest
Dividends
Gifts
Profits
Refunds
Insurance claims
  -medical
  -unemployment
Royalties
Rents
Pensions
Windfalls
. . . . ?
. . . . ?
. . . . ?

YOU

MONEY OUT

Taxes/Federal
Taxes/State
Taxes/County
Bank Accounts
  -Checking
  -Savings
Money Market Funds
Investments
House Payments/Rent
Insurance
Registration fees
Bills
  -utilities
  -department store
  -credit cards
Donations
Installment payments

1. Cross out every item in both columns that are *not* part of your life today.
2. Study the list and * the ones that bother you most.
3. Circle the items that have tax consequences and for which you do not have a satisfactory record-keeping process.

ACTION STEPS:

Questions, Questions, Questions

MONEY MINDER forms were developed to respond to specific questions. Look for the ones you need by reviewing this list.

☐ How diversified are my assets and how can I evaluate them?　　　p. 75

☐ What will my net profit or loss be if I decide to sell one of my stocks, bonds, or funds?　　　p. 33, 39, 45

☐ How can I calculate *when* to sell to protect gains?　　　p. 79

☐ How can I predict or plan for major fixed expenses as well as discretionary ones?　　　p. 57

☐ What's my approximate taxable income so far this year from all sources? Am I over- or underpaying on estimated taxes?　　　p. 83

☐ What are the dollar benefits so far in owning a home?　　　p. 81

☐ How are my portfolio investments doing so far this year?　　　p. 87

☐ How aggressive/conservative are my current portfolio investments? p. 89

☐ What is the total amount I invested last year and where? How much and where would I like to invest next year?　　　p. 85

☐ Where is everything I keep losing?　　　p. 96

☐ What were the earnings and profits in my mutual funds last year?　p. 49

☐ What personal possessions do I have? What are they worth and who do I want to have them?　　　p. 103

☐ What's my income property earning/losing and how much has it increased in value?　　　p. 91

☐ What information do I need to provide for tax purposes on a rental property?　　　p. 65

☐ Where will my retirement income come from?　　　p. 57

☐ What's in the safe deposit box—*now*?　　　p. 105

☐ What earnings are listed on my Social Security record? What benefits will I be receiving? How much can I earn without reducing them?　　　p. 59

☐ Which tax schedules/forms must I file this year? What records are needed?　　　p. 71

☐ What information do I need to collect and organize in order to develop a comprehensive financial plan?　　　p. 115

☐ What if I have a problem that doesn't fit any of the forms?　　　p. 116

In creating *your* **MONEY MINDER**, you need to consider not only where you are now, but where you are heading and how you want to get there.

If you don't know where you're going, it's hard to know if you've taken the right road, or even the right direction. You can choose before you start, or explore a bit and then decide. Goals do not limit you. They merely set a direction or destination that you are free to alter at any time. Think of it as a trip where you start out for Denver but might later decide to detour to Las Vegas and end up in Boston.

The first step is to place yourself on the map. Using your **NET WORTH** form (whichever you choose), establish some general destinations:

In 19_____ you are worth _____.

What would you like to be worth in 1 year? _____

3 years? _____   5 years? _____

Why did you choose those numbers? Rate the following motives for their importance to you (first, second, third or high, medium, low):

_____ Safety/Security

_____ Keep up with inflation (public and personal)

_____ Be able to do/buy certain things (house, trip, car, etc.)

_____ Feel in control

_____ See yourself as a smart investor

What *specific* uses will you have for money (beyond what you have now)?

Next year _____

_____

Next three years _____

_____

_____

Next five years _____

_____

What are you willing to do to get to your destination? How much time can/will you personally spend weekly _____ or monthly _____ bimonthly _____ ?

What resources are you willing to use?

☐ A tax preparation service
☐ A tax consultant
☐ A financial planner (once) on a fee basis
☐ A financial planner (periodically) on a fee basis
☐ A financial planner—for investment ideas

☐ Attorney—for wills
☐ CPA—for bookkeeping and/or tax preparation
☐ Financial planning courses. How many? _____
☐ Financial information services (newsletters, advisory services) How many? _____
☐ Books. How many? _____
☐ Magazines. Which?_____

You might not be ready to answer these questions right away. *Recognize that you are starting on your journey as soon as you begin to consider them seriously.* When you have some *preliminary* answers you are ready to create your first **GOALS** (see p. 17).

Many people are overwhelmed by trying to establish money goals yet most professionals will want you to create them first. For some of you, it might be more important to keep better track of what you are doing now and then generate goals based on what is realistic given your present circumstances and life-style. (see pp. 21, 23, 25).

Writing something down creates a different reality from just thinking about it. That's why career counselors, financial professionals, and personal journal advocates keep encouraging you to do so. Making your interior experience explicit is far more important in the world of money than most people are willing to admit. That also is why it will be useful after reading ''Where and How'' to write something here—even if it's only a feeling reaction like ''I'm not ready for this!'' or ''I don't have the time.''

Notes—for now _____

_____

_____

_____

_____

One Year: By _____

Destination ($) _____

Motives _____

Uses _____

Resources _____

Personal Effort _____

Move on to filling in the next two at your own pace. Keep looking at them. Some day you will be ready—perhaps sooner than you think!

Three Years: By _____

Destination ($) _____

Motives _____

Uses _____

Resources _____

Personal Effort _____

Five Years: By _____

Destination ($) _____

Motives _____

Uses _____

Resources _____

Personal Effort _____

►RECORDS MANAGEMENT FORMS

Month Oct, Nov, Dec, 1988

Source	Date	Amount: Constant	Periodic	Special
Salary	10/5	652		
	10/19	652		
Free lance Design	10/-		1,288	
Dividend	10/12		50	
Interest on c'King	10/21		6	
Birthday check	10/23			100
Medical Insurance	10/27			200
Salary	11/2	652		
	11/16	652		
Free lance Design	11/-		965	
Interest on cKing	11/26		9	
Salary	12/7	652		
	12/21	652		
Christmas Bonus	12/14			500
Free lance Design	12/-		1,020	
Christmas Checks	12/25			150
Interest on cKing	12/28		8	
TOTALS		3,912	3,346	950

Constant is for wages/salary, income you can count on from working or other sources.
Periodic is for interest, dividend income that you get from investing/saving on a consistent basis.
Special is for one-time, occasional windfalls—birthday checks, insurance claims, investment pay-outs, inheritance, etc.

I have always resisted formulas and budgets although I recognize they might be necessary for some folks who are in real financial distress. I think this format for getting a handle on where your money goes works well for most people who want to plug the leaks and fine tune their earning/spending process.

It starts with building a realistic database—i.e., what's going on now? Track your incoming $ on MONEY IN . . . (You'll probably need three months' worth—more if your sources of income are erratic.)

►MONEY IN

Source	Date	Amount:	Constant	Periodic	Special
	TOTALS				

Constant is for wages/salary, income you can count on from working or other sources.
Periodic is for interest, dividend income that you get from investing/saving on a consistent basis.
Special is for one-time, occasional windfalls—birthday checks, insurance claims, investment pay-outs, inheritance, etc.

Month **Oct., 1988**

Item	Date	Amount: Fixed	Necessary	Optional
Rent	10/1	675		
Cash	10/3			30
Phone	10/3			60
Car Repair	10/4		340	
Groceries	10/5		35	
Mastercard	10/6			64
Gas Credit Card	10/6		24	
Gas Credit Card	10/6		31	
Monthly Parking	10/8	35		
Groceries	10/10		40	
Cash	10/12			35
Medical Insurance (Extra)	10/14	50		
Gift	10/14			15
Haircut	10/19			20
Utilities	10/19		45	
Miscellaneous (House)	10/20		15	
Cash	10/20			30
Clothes (shoes)	10/22			60
Loan Payment	10/24		60	

Oct. continued →

TOTALS **760** **590** **314**

At the same time track on **MONEY OUT.** Try to pay by check or credit card so you create a record to refer to (check stubs, bills). For cash outlays track and record expenses of $5.00 or more. This won't be perfect but close enough. Group the rest as miscellaneous.

Month _____

Item	Date	Amount:	Fixed	Necessary	Optional

TOTALS_____

COMING IN	Certain	+	Pretty Sure	+	Possible	=	Total Income
	1775	+	1082	+	315	=	3172
							Monthly/Estimated

GOING OUT	Gross	Actual	Possible	Preferred
1. Housing		675		625
2. Heat/Light		45	40	45
3. Water		—		
4. Food		400	350*	
5. Phone		60	45	60
6. Taxes		260		
7. Loan Payments		60	0-soon!	0
8. Insurance *(Renters)*		10		
9. Maintenance—Home		50		
10. Maintenance—Personal		50		
11. Clothes		150	100	200
12. Transportation		265	?	200
13. Education				25
14. Recreation		250	200	
15. Medical *(includes extra ins.)*	110			
16. Vacations		100	80	100+
17. Contributions		15		25+
18. I.R.A.		125		334
19. Newspaper/Miscell.		96	80?	
20. Gifts		25	?	30+
		(2746)		

Notes * Take lunch at least three times a week

→ Start a fund for a down payment on a house ?? (3 years goal .....?)

© 1989 Michal E. Feder

Now you are ready to create an estimate that has a reasonable chance of working! Create your "Actual" current profile by listing all your outlays under one of the above categories and establishing a monthly average. (I prefer to work in months. You may prefer to record and average on a quarterly basis.) Create your "Possible" profile by looking hard at the categories you can and are willing to trim. Cut your phone bill? Turn down the heat? Eat out less? Use the "Preferred" column to establish an estimate that you would feel good about given your present financial circumstances. Thinking about your preferences opens up the possibilities for working to increase income to support the life-style you want. If you want a more complete item-by-item budget, there are many on the market. I have found them too tedious to finish. A simpler form completed is better than none at all!

	Certain +	Pretty Sure +	Possible =	Total Income
COMING IN	_____ +	_____ +	_____ =	_____
				Monthly/Estimated
GOING OUT	**Gross**	**Actual**	**Possible**	**Preferred**

1. Housing _____
2. Heat/Light _____
3. Water _____
4. Food _____
5. Phone _____
6. Taxes _____
7. Loan Payments _____
8. Insurance _____
9. Maintenance—Home _____
10. Maintenance—Personal _____
11. Clothes _____
12. Transportation _____
13. Education _____
14. Recreation _____
15. Medical _____
16. Vacations _____
17. Contributions _____
18. _____
19. _____
20. _____

Notes _____

_____

_____

Prepared 6/88

1. **Real Estate**
101 Memory Lane

Rockholme (⅓ interest)   Big City Rental

2. **Limited Partnerships**
Totals (10 in '88 - estimated value)

3. **Stocks**
Double Discount Acct.

Double Discount (Joint)

Big City Brokerage

Mexamerica Gas & Electric

Tri-State Banking

4. **Retirement**
Double Discount

New Times Fund

Uncle Sam Securities

Mt. States Securities Fund

5. **Annuities**
Rudder Insurance

Fair Play Insurance

6. **Savings Accounts (interest-bearing chekcing, money market, savings)**
Town Bank (Joint/House)

Town Bank (Personal)

Friendly S&L (Business Acct.)

Friendly S&L (Investment Acct.)

Big City S&L (Money Market)

7. **Commodities**
Big Gem Inc.

8. **Life Insurance**
Mid-Atlantic Mutual

Big Chief Mutual

To complete a form even as simple as **NET WORTH—AT A GLANCE,** *you will probably need a worksheet. Most of the information will come to you in the form of monthly statements over the next few weeks. Note the date and amount as they arrive. Then develop your own* **WORKSHEET** *form establishing categories and leaving a line for each source within the category. For example, I have two annuities and five separate savings accounts, so I allot two and five lines for those categories on my form. Make several copies of the form and experiment. Refer to* **NET WORTH—IN DETAIL** *for possible categories. When your form reflects your current situation, make a master for future use. Photocopy worksheets periodically and leave with a friend or store elsewhere. Be prepared to outgrow your worksheet as your assets increase. Use the master in* **MONEY MINDER** *to reformat when necessary.*

1. Real Estate

_____

2. Limited Partnerships

_____

3. Stocks

_____

_____

_____

_____

4. Retirement

_____

_____

_____

5. Annuities

_____

6. Savings Accounts (interest-bearing chekcing, money market, savings)

_____

_____

_____

7. Commodities

_____

8. Life Insurance

_____

_____

Prepared **3/88**

ASSETS

Home (estimated value)	270,000(E)
Cash (checking accounts)	300
Other Real Estate (estimated value)	—
Interest-bearing (savings, T-bills, money market accounts)	500
Investments (stocks, bonds, limited partnerships)	9,000(E)
Possessions (car, furniture, jewelry, equipment)	15,000
Retirement (IRA, Keogh, pension plans)	3,000
Life Insurance (cash value)	—

TOTAL ASSETS **297,800**

LIABILITIES

Mortgages (current balance)	200,000
Car, Furniture, Equipment Loans	6,800
Credit Card, Charge Accounts (if total over $1,000)	
Personal Loans	

TOTAL LIABILITIES **206,800**

ASSETS: **297,800**   minus LIABILITIES: **206,800** = **91,000**
Current NET WORTH

© 1989 Michal E. Feder

*When my son tried **NET WORTH—AT A GLANCE** he noticed that he and his wife owned a lot of valuable art work they hadn't considered assets. I encouraged him to make an inventory as his second step right away while it was still in his mind. The logical time to start on the INSURANCE inventory (p.67) might be the next time you have to pay a premium and the records are all out in front of you. Then keep adding each policy to the inventory as you make a payment. By the end of the year you will be up and running and not have suffered through the frustration of searching out each policy and extracting the basic information. Under life insurance, cash value is listed since you might want to tap it while you're alive. It might also be important for you to check your policy and note what your heirs will actually collect.*

ASSETS

Home (estimated value) _____

Cash (checking accounts) _____

Other Real Estate (estimated value) _____

Interest-bearing (savings, T-bills, money market accounts) _____

Investments (stocks, bonds, limited partnerships) _____

Possessions (car, furniture, jewelry, equipment) _____

Retirement (IRA, Keogh, pension plans) _____

Life Insurance (cash value) _____

_____ _____

TOTAL ASSETS ═══════════

LIABILITIES

Mortgages (current balance) _____

Car, Furniture, Equipment Loans _____

Credit Card, Charge Accounts (if total over $1,000) _____

Personal Loans _____

_____ _____

TOTAL LIABILITIES ═══════════

ASSETS:_____ minus LIABILITIES:_____ = ═══════════

CURRENT NET WORTH

Prepared _7/88_

ASSETS

1. **Cash:** checking, savings accounts, unused traveler's checks, under the rug, etc. _1800_

2. **Securities:** stocks, bonds, T-bills, funds _50,000_

3. **Limited Partnerships:** real estate, R&D, leasing, oil & gas, etc. _45,000_

4. **Life Insurance:** cash surrender value _5,000_

5. **Retirement Accounts:** IRA, Keogh, annuities _35,000_

6. **Pension Plan** _—_

7. **Home:** estimated value _170,000_

8. **Vehicles:** car, motor home, boats, trailers _16,500_

9. **Other Real Estate:** summer home, land, private placements _25,000_

10. **Receivables:** .accounts, notes, rents, royalties _12,000_

11. **Refunds Due:** deposits, tax refunds, rebates _—_

12. **Other Assets:** _10,000_

    Home furnishings, appliances _2,500_

    Art/antiques/jewelry/furs _750_

    Sports/hobby equipment _5,000_

    Trade/professional equipment _—_

    Memberships, interests in investment clubs, etc. ____?

    Other: _____ **TOTAL ASSETS** _378,550_

LIABILITIES

1. **Real Estate:** balance on mortgages _35,000_

2. **Contracts Payable:** car, appliances, etc. _—_

3. **Accounts Payable:** credit cards, department stores _350_

4. **Notes Payable:** loans _—_

5. **Taxes Due:** state, federal, property, Social Security (for self-employed) **9/15** _1,500_

6. **Other:** _College Tuition - due 9/1_ ____? _2,100_

    TOTAL LIABILITIES _38,950_

ASSETS: _378,550_ minus LIABILITIES: _38,950_ = _339,600_

Current NET WORTH

I have found "Other Assets" (Item 12) in **NET WORTH—IN DETAIL** *the toughest to itemize. You can guess and take your chances in case of fire, storm, theft, etc., or you can document. The easiest way is one room at a time. Sit in the middle and look around. Make a laundry list, lump the minor assets, and value the others broadly at 25%, 50%, or 75% of cost depending age (except antiques and jewelry). Hint: One room a day or week is better than trying to do it all at once and quitting midstream. Or, take photos of everything of some value. Note year purchased and cost on the back of the photos. Store them in your safe deposit box. Add photos as you accumulate more valuables. Also check with your insurance agent for what your policy requires in documenting a loss.* **PERSONAL PROPERTY** *(p. 103) creates a worksheet for this form.*

ASSETS

  1. **Cash:** checking, savings accounts, unused traveler's checks,

     under the rug, etc. _____

  2. **Securities:** stocks, bonds, T-bills, funds _____

  3. **Limited Partnerships:** real estate, R&D, leasing, oil & gas, etc. _____

  4. **Life Insurance:** cash surrender value _____

  5. **Retirement Accounts:** IRA, Keogh, annuities _____

  6. **Pension Plan** _____

  7. **Home:** estimated value _____

  8. **Vehicles:** car, motor home, boats, trailers _____

  9. **Other Real Estate:** summer home, land, private placements _____

10. **Receivables:** accounts, notes, rents, royalties _____

11. **Refunds Due:** deposits, tax refunds, rebates _____

12. **Other Assets:**

     Home furnishings, appliances _____

     Art/antiques/jewelry/furs _____

     Sports/hobby equipment _____

     Trade/professional equipment _____

     Memberships, interests in investment clubs, etc. _____

     Other: _____ ? _____

                                  TOTAL ASSETS _____

LIABILITIES

  1. **Real Estate:** balance on mortgages _____

  2. **Contracts Payable:** car, appliances, etc. _____

  3. **Accounts Payable:** credit cards, department stores _____

  4. **Notes Payable:** loans _____

  5. **Taxes Due:** state, federal, property, Social Security (for self-employe _____

  6. **Other:** _____ ? _____

                         TOTAL LIABILITIES _____

ASSETS: _____ minus **LIABILITIES:** _____ = _____

                                       Current NET WORTH

Owner _Self_

TRADE DATE	TRANSACTION DESCRIPTION								SETTLEMENT DATE 3/29/83

TRADE DATE
3/21/83

SETTLEMENT DATE
3/29/83
061394401
SECURITY NUMBER

YOU BOUGHT
FLAIR GRAPHICS INC

NET AMOUNT
2,050.00

T	AB	QUANTITY	PRICE	PRINCIPAL AMOUNT
06A		100	20 ½	2,050.00

DD IS MARKET MAKER

REFERENCE
1356681

IDA SMART
101 MEMORY LANE
BIG CITY, CA 94104

DOUBLE DISCOUNT INC
101 FRONT STREET
BIG CITY, CA 94109

ACCOUNT NO. 114-863508-0-55

357488

On other than round lots (normally 100 shares) on most exchanges an amount may be added to the price on purchases or deducted on sales. An explanation will be provided on request. Please advise your account executive immediately if this information does not agree with your records or if you have any questions.

EARNINGS/DISTRIBUTIONS

Year	Dividends	Cap. Gains
1983	96	
1984	145	
"	2 for 1 stock split	
1985	180	
1986	248	320
1987	75	
"	SOLD →	5/87

Original Cost 2,050
Additions
6/29 2 for 1 split + 50 sh-
no cost

11/30/79 + 50 sh. 1,042

Net Cost _3,092_

Objectives/reason for purchase:
leading position in growing
field (T.V. graphics), low P/E
steady earnings, 50-100%
increase 3-4 years

*This form saves untold time and frustration looking for, copying, and keeping track of buy and sell slips. Depending upon how many stocks you own and how often you trade, you might find it useful to transfer your gains and losses to **STOCK SALES—SUMMARY**, pages (p.37), as the year goes along. The running totals will not be sufficient for final tax preparation, but provide key information in the fourth quarter for adjusting your final tax payment, considering investments with different tax benefits, or deciding if and when to take losses on stocks, bonds, bad debts, etc.*

GLUE CONFIRMATION OF PURCHASE HERE

EARNINGS/DISTRIBUTIONS

Year	Dividends	Cap. Gains

Original Cost _____

Additions _____

_____

_____

_____

_____

_____

_____

_____

_____

_____

Net Cost _____

Objectives/reason for purchase:

_____

_____

_____

_____

					SETTLEMENT DATE 5/20/87

TRANSACTION DESCRIPTION

061394401
SECURITY NUMBER

TRADE DATE
5/13/87

YOU SOLD
FLAIR GRAPHICS INC

NET AMOUNT
7,121 16

T AB	QUANTITY	PRICE	PRINCIPAL AMOUNT	COMMISSION FEE	
06A	200	36	7,200.00	78.60	.24

DD IS MARKET MAKER

REFERENCE
1824983

IDA SMART
101 MEMORY LANE
BIG CITY, CA 94104

DOUBLE DISCOUNT INC
101 FRONT STREET
BIG CITY, CA 94109

ACCOUNT NO. 114-863508-0-55

360260

On other than round lots (normally 100 shares) on most exchanges an amount may be added to the price on purchases or deducted on sales. An explanation will be provided on request. Please advise your account executive immediately if this information does not agree with your records or if you have any questions.

Total Cost __3,092__
(Remember to include reinvested
dividends and capital gains)

Total Return __7121__

Net (Gain)Loss __4029__
☒ Long term   ☐ Short term

Notes: *130% gain/annualized 31%*
Recent run-up in price
P/E now above market
averages.. goals met
→ watch and repurchase?

© 1989 Michal E. Feder

Buying and selling stocks requires a discipline few possess. The hardest decision is not what to buy, but when to sell. Few experts are any better at it than the rest of us. The **STOCK** form keeps you focused. It encourages you to quantify the results expected. The objective can always be amended upward. It also reveals in a simple and glaring fashion which stocks are really producing the best total return. I photocopy my stock form with purchase information on the front and sale on the back. I like the idea of having the complete record on a single sheet of paper. One sheet per stock is more compact. Two would provide space on the back of each for additional comments and reminders. See **CREATING A STOP** (p. 79) for another way to decide when to sell.

GLUE CONFIRMATION OF SALE HERE

Total Cost _____
　　(Remember to include reinvested
　　dividends and capital gains)

Total Return _____

Net Gain/Loss _____
　　☐ Long term　　☐ Short term

Notes:

_____
_____
_____
_____
_____
_____
_____
_____

Prepared _12/87_ Tax Year _1987_

Stock	Sold	ST Gain	LT Gain	ST Loss	LT Loss
1 Ar Office Supply	3/29			− 1745 *	
2 Dec T-Bond	7/5	+518			
3 Central Banking	8/24		+1150		
4 Fund 1 → Fund 2 (Transfer)	9/2		+1079		
5 Down East Bk.	12/8		+1519		
6 Safety First	12/16				−90
7 Homestyle Mining	12/16				−105
8 Ark Paper	12/16				−235
9					
10 Totals for '87		+518	+3748	− 1745	− 430
11					
12					
13					
14					
15					
16					

Notes/Reminders _* Set stop losses and stick to them!_
Get rid of stocks that don't move sooner.

*This is a handy form if you sell stocks during the year which will create tax consequences. By keeping a running total of the net amounts—losses and gains, short- and long-term—as they accumulate, you can take into account the tax benefits of a sale at any time. This has helped me discipline myself to take long-term profits at appropriate times as well as monitor and accept losses. It is also useful in tracking to estimate taxes. As an entrepreneur with a variable income, which year I decide to sell can make a difference. In years when I have had healthy gains through stock sales, I look for losses or expenses and deductions to offset them. This kind of choosing is not possible without a clear record. The totals are lifted from the **STOCK** forms or estimated before a decision. It is worth it to me to separate these totals from the details necessary for tax returns.*

Stock	Sold	ST Gain	LT Gain	ST Loss	LT Loss
1					
2					
3					
4					
5					
6					
7					
8					
9					
10					
11					
12					
13					
14					
15					
16					

Notes/Reminders _____

_____

_____

_____

_____

Owner _____

	TRANSACTION DESCRIPTION		SETTLEMENT DATE 3/29/84

TRADE DATE
3/21/84

YOU BOUGHT
CENTRAL COUNTY POLL.
7.25 DUE 9/1/00(CALLABLE 9/1/90)

061394401
SECURITY NUMBER

PRINCIPAL AMOUNT

NET AMOUNT
. 10,500:00

T	AB	QUANTITY	PRICE

06A 10M 100.5

DD IS MARKET MAKER

REFERENCE
1356681

IDA SMART
101 MEMORY LANE
BIG CITY, CA 94104

DOUBLE DISCOUNT INC
101 FRONT STREET
BIG CITY, CA 94109

ACCOUNT NO. 114-863508-0-55

357488

On other than round lots (normally 100 shares) on most exchanges an amount may be added to the price on purchases or deducted on sales. An explanation will be provided on request. Please advise your account executive immediately if this information does not agree with your records or if you have any questions.

Cost **10,500**

EARNINGS

Year	Interest
6/84	362.50
12/84	362.50
6/85	362.50
12/85	362.50
6/86	362.50
12/86	362.50
	$2,175

Objectives/Reasons for Purchase
Safety - income

Conversion Features: _____

Callable at *face* after **7** years

Tax Status: Nonexempt _____ Exempt (Federal) _____ Exempt (state) _____

© 1989 Michal E. Feder

*With interest rates fluctuating as they have in recent years, bonds are being traded more and more like stocks instead of being tucked away until maturity as in the past. This form works equally well for long-term investors and would-be traders. The special features of your bond can be checked off at the bottom within easy reach. Use **BOND PURCHASE** also to track interest payments and follow-up if, as occasionally happens, your check doesn't arrive.*

PASTE CONFIRMATION OF PURCHASE HERE

EARNINGS

Year	Interest

Cost _____

Objectives/Reasons for Purchase

_____

_____

_____

Conversion Features: _____ **Callable at** _____ **after** _____ **years**

Tax Status: Nonexempt _____ **Exempt (Federal)** _____ **Exempt (state)** _____

```
                                                          SETTLEMENT DATE
                                                            5/20/87
                            TRANSACTION DESCRIPTION          061394401
                                                          SECURITY NUMBER
 TRADE DATE
 5/13/87     YOU SOLD
             CENTRAL COUNTY POLL.
             7.25 DUE 9/1/00(CALLABLE 9/1/90)              NET AMOUNT

 T AB  QUANTITY    PRICE      PRINCIPAL AMOUNT  COMMISSION  FEE          9,414:00
 06A   10M          93                          113.50     .50

             DD IS MARKET MAKER


 REFERENCE                                  DOUBLE DISCOUNT INC
 1824983   IDA SMART                        101 FRONT STREET
           101 MEMORY LANE                  BIG CITY,CA 94109
           BIG CITY, CA 94104

 ACCOUNT NO  114-863508-0-55                          360260
```

On other than round lots (normally 100 shares) on most exchanges an amount may be added to the price on purchases or deducted on sales. An explanation will be provided on request. Please advise your account executive immediately if this information does not agree with your records or if you have any questions

Cost ___10,500___

Net Sales Price ___9,414___

Net Gain/(Loss) ___−1,086___

☐ Long term ☐ Short term

9,414 - sale 5/20/87
2,175 - Interest earned 6/84-5/87
413 - Tax saving on loss in '87
―――
12,002
−10,500 - cost
―――
1,502
−805 - Taxes paid on interest earned '84-'87
"real" → 697 net profit

Notes:
Interest rates up
Bond value declining

© 1989 Michal E. Feder

As with other sales of securities, calculating your net return at the time you sell when all the transaction slips are in front of you takes only a few minutes—and will mean one less thing to worry about at tax time. My notes on the lower left show you how I would use the open space on the form to analyze this transaction.

40

GLUE CONFIRMATION OF SALE/TRANSFER HERE

Cost _____

Net Sales Price _____

Net Gain/Loss _____

☐ Long term ☐ Short term

Notes:

_____

_____

_____

_____

_____

_____

_____

_____

_____

Prepared __6/88__ Owner __Joint__

Name	Coupon Rate	Face Value	Maturity	Cost	Current Yield
1 Pub Service	11.40	10,000	3/1/00	7998	14.3
2 Downtown Muni.	10.58	10,000	6/15/05	8300	12.7
3 General Ltg.	9.50	10,000	7/1/90	8800	9.50
4 U.S. Oil *	13.	10,000	1/1/00	11,700	11.1
5 County Hosp.	7.75	10,000	7/1/16	9,750	7.78
6					
7					
8					
9					
10					
11					
12					
13					
14					
15					

Notes: __* Callable at face value after 11/1/92__

If you own individual bonds, this form provides a simple record and a chance to evaluate your bonds as a group. Whatever your reasons for owning bonds, it is important to pay attention to how they are producing so you can easily compare them with other investment possibilities.

Coupon Rate is the interest quoted on the face of the bond. Current Yield is a more important measure for you. It is the actual return you are getting and might be higher or lower depending on whether you bought the bond at a discount (below face) or a premium (above). To calculate it multiply the coupon rate of each bond by its face value and divide by your cost. Remember that if current yield on any bond is lower than its coupon rate, the price at which you could sell it will be higher than your original cost.

Name	Coupon Rate	Face Value	Maturity	Cost	Current Yield
1 _____					_____
2 _____					_____
3 _____					_____
4 _____					_____
5 _____					_____
6 _____					_____
7 _____					_____
8 _____					_____
9 _____					_____
10 _____					_____
11 _____					_____
12 _____					_____
13 _____					_____
14 _____					_____
15 _____					_____

Notes:_____

_____

_____

_____

_____

Owner *Self*

Name *Midwest Fund* Fund No. *2*   Acct. No. *001008990* *5/85*

Tel. Transfer to *CASH FUND*   Customer Service *800-XXX-0234*

Trading *800-XXX-0X0X*   Hours *Central Standard 9 to 6*

Redemption Requirements *Signature guarantee* On file ✓ *6/84*

MIDWEST FUND   101 FRONT ST.   RIVER CITY, WI 54022

CONFIRMATION

| ☒ Initial Purchase | ☐ Repeat Purchase | ☐ Redemption |
| ☐ Reinvestment of Dividend | ☐ Reinvestment of Capital Gain | ☐ Transfer |

| SHARES | | CERTIFICATE | SHARES HELD | | TOTAL |
PREVIOUSLY HELD	THIS TRANSACTION		OPEN ACCOUNT		
-0-	41.982	-0-	41.982		41.982

June 17, 1984
ACCEPTANCE DATE

| PRICE | | AMOUNT RECEIVED | AMOUNT DUE | | |
PER SHARE	AGGREGATE		FUND, INC. (1)	INVESTOR (2)	
$23.82	$1,000.00	$1,000.00	-0-	-0-	

PAYMENT DATE

(1) REMITTANCE DUE WITHIN SEVEN (7) BUSINESS DAYS AFTER ACCEPTANCE OF ORDER.
MAKE CHECK PAYABLE TO: MidwestFUND, INC.
(2) AMOUNT DUE INVESTOR WILL BE MAILED DIRECT FROM THE FUND'S CUSTODIAN:
CENTRAL BANK & TRUST COMPANY

PLAN
☐ A   ☐ B
☒ C   ☐ D

INVESTOR:

IDA SMART
101 MEMORY LANE
BIG CITY, CA 94104

EARNINGS / DISTRIBUTIONS / REINVESTED

Year	Dividends	Cap Gains	
1984	62		62
"		26	26
1985	82		82
"		130	130
"		96	96
			396

Original Cost   *1,000*
Additions   *1,000*
Reinvested   *396*

Net Cost   *2,396*

Objectives/reason for purchase:
medium risk - good, young manager, medium size, well diversified - U.S. only

*Originally I used my **STOCK** forms (pp. 33, 35, 37) for mutual funds as well. If you only have a few funds and do little or no trading or exchanging, the **STOCK** forms might be all you need. But the market place is changing rapidly and investors in no load funds especially tend to be more active in managing them than in the past. If you are a no load investor, the information at the top of this form will be invaluable.*

Be sure to keep it in pencil or erasable pen. New phone services, investor service lines, and account numbers change so often I have started noting the date of each entry!

Name_____ Fund No_____ Acct. No_____

  Tel. Transfer to_____ Customer Service_____

Trading_____ Hours_____

Redemption Requirements_____ On file_____

GLUE CONFIRMATION OF ORIGINAL PURCHASE HERE

EARNINGS / DISTRIBUTIONS / REINVESTED

Year	Dividends	Cap Gains

Original Cost _____

   Additions _____

Objectives/reason for purchase:

Net Cost _____

MIDWEST FUND   101 FRONT ST.   RIVER CITY,   WI 54022

C O N F I R M A T I O N

| [X] Initial Purchase | [ ] Repeat Purchase | [ ] Redemption |
| [ ] Reinvestment of Dividend | [ ] Reinvestment of Capital Gain | [X] Transfer |

SHARES		SHARES HELD			June 17, 1984
PREVIOUSLY HELD	THIS TRANSACTION	CERTIFICATE	OPEN ACCOUNT	TOTAL	ACCEPTANCE DATE
-0-	97	-0-	97	97	

PRICE		AMOUNT RECEIVED	AMOUNT DUE		9/22/85
PER SHARE	AGGREGATE		CASH FUND, INC. (1)	INVESTOR (2)	PAYMENT DATE
$28.76	$2790.00		$2790.00	-0-	

(1) REMITTANCE DUE WITHIN SEVEN (7) BUSINESS DAYS AFTER ACCEPTANCE OF ORDER.
       MAKE CHECK PAYABLE TO: Midwest FUND, INC.
(2) AMOUNT DUE INVESTOR WILL BE MAILED DIRECT FROM THE FUND'S CUSTODIAN:
       CENTRAL BANK & TRUST COMPANY

PLAN

| [ ] A | [ ] B |
| [X] C | [ ] D |

INVESTOR:

IDA SMART
101 MEMORY LANE
BIG CITY, CA 94104

Total Cost _____ **2,396**
(Remember to include reinvested
dividends and capital gains)

Total Return _____ **2,790**

Net Gain/Loss _____ **394**
[✓] Long term   [ ] Short term

Notes: **was lagging market**

9/17/85 Transfer to **CASH FUND** _____ **195** **14.25** **2,970**
Date   Shares   Price per Sh.   Total $

for purchase of **2,970** _____ **1** _____ **2,970**
                          Shares   Price per Sh.   Total $

One of the conveniences computers have brought to investing is the simplicity and speed with which transactions can occur. The availability of telephone transfer and written redemption procedures have made it relatively easy for mutual fund investors to, in effect, become their own brokers. And guess who gets to verify the accuracy of these activities!

*To save time deciphering confirmations that show up five days to a week later, I note the exact number of shares, price per share and total $'s going out and the same information for the fund it's going into at the bottom of my **SALE/TRANSFER** form. This can be especially helpful in tracking movement into an existing account. It's like going through the woods on a hike. You leave simple markers along the way to help you retrace your steps when necessary.*

GLUE CONFIRMATION OF SALE/TRANSFER HERE

Total Cost _____
(Remember to include reinvested
    dividends and capital gains)

Total Return _____

Net Gain/Loss _____
    ☐ Long term   ☐ Short term

Notes:

_____

_____

_____

_____

_____ **Transfer to** _____   _____ _____ _____
Date   Shares   Price per Sh.   Total $

               for purchase of _____ _____ _____
                                   Shares   Price per Sh.   Total $

19 __88__

NAME	Starting Value	Additions	Reinvested	Earnings	Mid-year Value	Year-end Value
Far East	2583			227	3,081	2797
Healthcare	1,738			23	2,461	2,140
Midwest	9,631		←	2,998	10,634	11,078
New Fund	6,666 +2,000		←	507	10,015	9,448
Old Glory	28,670		←	5,275	33,544	34,752
	49,228		8,780			60,215

Notes Far East to money market 11/18
Old Glory up 21% — add to position next
year?
New Fund +782 (11.73%)

Designing a simple *form that highlights crucial information is a challenge. When you get one that works it's fun. This has become one of my favorites. The questions I ask myself are: what's a workable time frame, is the information readily available, and will the picture the record presents be clear and useful?*

This form shows the total $ any or all funds earned, total $ added, total $ reinvested, and total return for each or all investments. (Subtract additions made during the year from year-end value to get a more accurate estimate of real growth.) To generate a % or rate of return, subtract starting from year-end value and divide that number into starting value.

This form works well for investors who are managing a group of mutual funds the way they would a stock bond portfolio, but can be used for any combination.

NAME	Starting Value	Additions	Reinvested	Earnings	Mid-year Value	Year-end Value

Notes _____

_____

_____

Prepared **2/88** Tax Year **1988** Owner **Joint**

	Name/ Certificate No.	Location	Face Value	Interest Rate	Unit Cost	Maturing
1	Vinehaven Bk	metal Box	10,000	7.85	4,000	12/14/88
2	Bay City S+L	Safe Dep.	10,000	7.42	1,000	9/19/88
3	City Savings Fd.	Safe Dep.	5,000	0	376.81	4/22/94 →
4	20th C. S+L ←		10,000	8.0	10,000	8/15/88
5	" ←		3,000	7.0	1,000	11/10/88
6	"	Safe Dep.	20,000	9.0	10,000	6/16/88
7						
8						
9						
10						
11						
12						
13						
14						
15						
16						
17						

TOTALS: Maturing in

January	May	September 10,000 + Int.
February	June 20,000 + Int.	October
March	July	November 3,000 + Int.
April	August 10,000 + Int.	December 10,000 + Int.

© 1989 Michal E. Feder

Although I do not maintain a portfolio of CDs, I was encouraged to include this form in MONEY MINDER for those who do. The top of the page is for basic information. The bottom was designed to alert you to when and how much you will be receiving for spending or reinvesting. To avoid confusion, set up a form for each calendar year, list the CD in the year purchased, and carry forward the amount at maturity to the appropriate year and month.

	Name/ Certificate No.	Location	Face Value	Interest Rate	Unit Cost	Maturing
1						
2						
3						
4						
5						
6						
7						
8						
9						
10						
11						
12						
13						
14						
15						
16						
17						

TOTALS: Maturing in

January	_____	May	_____	September	_____
February	_____	June	_____	October	_____
March	_____	July	_____	November	_____
April	_____	August	_____	December	_____

Name _Everyman's Equity (REIT)_ ► LIMITED PARTNERSHIPS

Owner _Self_   Account No. _60599_   Units _10_

	Date	Amount
Initial Investment:	6/23/79	$ 5,000
	10/9/80	5,000
Additions:		1,028
		725
		1,170
		1,029

EARNINGS RECORD

Date	Dividends/ Distributions	Cashed	Reinvested	Tax Benefits
1979		133		
1980		178		
1981		446		
1982		1,285		
1983		1,393		
1984	1,284	256	1,028	
1985	948	223	725	244 non taxable
1986	1,577	407	1,170	
1987	1,029	4,321	1,029	
1988	245 1/31		3,952	
	278 4/12			

Invested to Date: $ 13,952

Return to Date: 8,273

Estimated Value: $ 15,582 in '87

Rate of Return (Annualized):   6.62 %

LIMITED PARTNERSHIPS was born when I started to invest in limited partnerships and wanted to have a record of distributions that also included tax benefits and estimated appreciation as time went on. Sometimes it helps me in deciding whether to reinvest dividends or place them elsewhere. For partnerships that do not permit reinvestment, it has helped me decide whether to invest in another program by the same management group. I update the evaluation section periodically in pencil or erasable pen and keep the rest as an ongoing track.

Owner_____ Account No._____ Units_____

	Date	Amount
Initial Investment:	_____	_____
Additions:	_____	_____
	_____	_____
	_____	_____
	_____	_____
	_____	_____
	_____	_____

EARNINGS RECORD

Date	Dividends/ Distributions	Cashed	Reinvested	Tax Benefits

Invested to Date: $_____

Return to Date: _____

Estimated Value: $_____

Rate of Return (Annualized):   _____%

Prepared **6/88**   Owner **Spouse**

Tax Year	Investment	Amount	Date	Ded / Non-Ded
1981	Downtown S+L	1500	2/81	1,500
1982	New Times Fund.	1500	8/82	1,500
1983	Double Discount	2,000	10/83	2,000 – Fed. 1,500 – State
1984	"	1,000 1,000	11/12/84 3/24/85	2,000 – Fed. 1,500 – State
1985	"	2,000	4/10/86	2,000 – Fed. 1,500 – State
1986	New Times Fund. Uncle Sam Securities	1,000 1,000 1,000	6/15/86 11/3/86	2,000 – Fed. 1,500 – State
1987	New Times	1,000 940	9/10/87 3/27/88	2,000 – Fed. 2,000 – State

* $2,369 transferred 3/83 to Double Discount Account

CURRENT BOX SCORE

Investment	Invested to Date	Current Value
New Times	4,440	9,200
Double Discount	4,500	8,045
	2,369 (transfer)	3,046
		1,130
Uncle Sam Securities	1,000	
	Total Current Value	21,021
	6/88	

RETIREMENT IN is a three-way form. Record all your contributions from year to year in one place. Track partial contributions made at different times, especially because they can be made the following year for the previous tax year. Use the deductible column to track differences between federal and state allowances and contributions that are tax deferred but not tax deductible under The 1986 Tax Reform Act. This will become invaluable in the future when you start making withdrawals and want to be taxed correctly on these differing contributions. The bottom of the page can be used to evaluate your entire program or compare different IRA accounts to decide on next year's contribution. This form works for Keoghs and other self-directed pension plans too.

Tax Year	Investment	Amount	Date	Ded / Non-Ded

CURRENT BOX SCORE

Investment	Invested to Date	Current Value

Total Current Value_____

Year __1988__ Owner __Joint__

Source	Date	Amount	Notes Annual
Social Security (spouse) monthly		960	11,520
Pension "		600	7,200
IRA "		333	3,996 Draw out earnings only
Dividend Income (E) "		625	7,500 *
Interest (E)		250	3,000
C.D.'s 50,000 @ 7.2% "		300	3,600

Notes __* continue to reinvest as much dividend income as possible__

© 1989 Michal E. Feder

Investments made today in anticipation of retirement will generate a need for a new kind of record. The days of relying on Social Security, pensions, or a combination are disappearing, especially for large numbers of job changers and those who are self-employed. Retirement income is likely to come from a variety of sources: Social Security, pension plans, IRAs and Keoghs, annuities, dividends, interest, loans from single-premium life policies, and sales of other assets.

Each of these sources will be providing you with year-end totals for tax purposes. This form is to forecast and plan based on known sources such as Social Security and required withdrawals such as IRAs. Then you can decide where else you want to draw from to meet your desired income needs. The idea is to withdraw only what you need and keep as much as possible invested and growing.

Source	Date	Amount	Notes

Notes _____

_____

_____

_____

Owner _Self_   No _XOX - OO - XXOX_   ▶ *SOCIAL SECURITY*

Quarters needed _37_   Requirement met _✔_ Local Office _444-66X6_

Year	Covered Earnings	Monthly Benefit	Allowed Earnings
1983	31,325		
1984	34,619		
1985	35,522		
1986	37,411		
1987	39,219		
1988	→	680	6,100

Notes _1983- Requested update_
1987-   "   "   & benefits estimate
1988- Applied January - Benefits start
2nd month after birthday

© 1989 Michal E. Feder

On the Social Security earnings record are these words: ". . . *report any errors right away because the law only allows us to correct a Social Security record within a limited period of time . . . usually 3 years, 3 months and 15 days after the year in which the error occurs . . .*" In other words, if they have the wrong numbers and you don't correct them, you might not get all the benefits you've earned. The new (1988) verification form groups earned income for prior years by year. Verifying the record is important if your income varies from year to year, includes employment and self-employment income, or have had to file amended returns.

Request an update every 3 years and check it against your tax returns. The new form also includes benefits estimates. Once you start receiving benefits, you can record changes from year to year, and the earnings limits set for ages 62–70.

Owner _____ No _____   ► *SOCIAL SECURITY*

Quarters needed _____ Requirement met ____ Local Office _____

Year	Covered Earnings	Monthly Benefit	Allowed Earnings

Notes _____

_____

_____

Prepared 4/86

Address 101 Memory Lane

Owner Joint ownership

Purchase Price 177,000

Closing Costs 1,865

5/85 Total 178,865

Capital Improvements	Year	Cost	Location of Records
Paneling (Living rm)	1986	1500	Metal Box
Deck	1987	900	"
New Kitchen Counters	1988	1,100	with tax info checks for '88

Year	Maintenance	Taxes	Tax Benefits mortgage & int.	Value (Estimate)
1986	500	1,800	4,550	179,000
1987	750	1,920	4,517	184,000
1988	900	1,985	4,480	191,000

PROJECTIONS

Rate of Appreciation: Maintenance @ 25% a yr.

Taxes @ 5% a yr.

Tax Benefits 1,500 + a yr.

Value of Property + 8% in 3 yrs.

Notes/Reminders 1/88 – consolidate maintenance records and improvement receipts in '88!

HOME collects basic information in one form so it won't get buried in an inaccessible file folder. The key piece that many people neglect is capital improvements. It's easy to lose track of which year you redid the kitchen or added the deck, but these costs can add up to a healthy amount when establishing a cost basis when you sell. Use it also to alert yourself to capital expenses looming on the horizon and what it is really costing you each year to be a homeowner. When you run out of space, just make another copy from your master and continue.

Prepared _____

Address _____ **Purchase Price** _____

Owner _____ **Closing Costs** _____

Total _____

Capital Improvements	Year	Cost	Location of Records
_____			
_____			
_____			
_____			
_____			
_____			

Year	Maintenance	Taxes	Tax Benefits	Value (Estimate)
_____				
_____				
_____				
_____				

PROJECTIONS

Rate of Appreciation: Maintenance _____

Taxes _____

Tax Benefits _____

Value of Property _____

Notes/Reminders _____

_____

Prepared __10/84__

Description __Lakeside (summer home)__
Owner __1⁄3 ownership__   Date Inherited __5/68__
Starting Value __80,000__
(Set at time of transfer) LAND __150,000__   Based On __current lake front prices perft.__
Current Value   HOUSE __50,000__

Year	Maintenance Family Shares	Capital Expenses Totals	Taxes	Tax Benefits 1⁄3 Share
1972	575	Dock - 800	429	143
1975	680	Legal 878 Survey 277	756	252
1980	1,500	Painting 937 Heater 470 etc.	1,530	510
1981	1,300	totals 2007 Upholstery - 400	1,768	589
1982	1,350		2,006	668
1983	1,100		2,139	713
1984	1,150	carpets 175 Motor/Boat 150	2,236	745
1986	1,600	Dish washer > 1,352 Tree Pruning	2,623	874
1987	1,800	876	3,062*	1,020

PROJECTIONS

Rate of Appreciation (Expenses) __5 year average 1280__

Rate of Appreciation (Value) __Taxes up 50% in 5 years__

Future Capital Expenses __Dock (partial in '85) new sailboat '86?__

Future Uses/Notes __Assessments updated in 1968.__

__coming up again...?__

__* new assessment - ugh! / check current value in '88__

INHERITANCE has helped me consolidate information on some property I inherited and coown with my brother and sister. Since we want to keep it in the family, it's useful to have a record all on one sheet of paper of what it has been costing me— and what it is likely to cost in the future. As the taxes rise inexorably, it's a small comfort to be reminded of the amount deductible from my taxes each year.

Description _____

Owner _____

Starting Value _____   **Date Inherited** _____
(Set at time of transfer)

Current Value _____   **Based On** _____

Year	Maintenance	Capital Expenses	Taxes	Tax Benefits

PROJECTIONS

Rate of Appreciation (Expenses) _____

Rate of Appreciation (Value) _____

Future Capital Expenses _____

Future Uses/Notes _____

_____

_____

_____

Year _1988_ Location _Big City_

Gross Income: _7,900 (E)_ % of Ownership: _40%_ Net Income: _?_

EXPENSES:	Fees	Mortgage (Interest)	Maintenance	Utilities	Auto (Travel)
		3,312			
1/1→6/1					
2/8 Pest Spraying			55		
2/88 Roof repair			360		
3/88 Drainage repair			120		
garbage			15		
4/88 Advertising 142					
5/88 Deadbolting/Rekey			85		
1/1 - 6/1 21 trips					189
6/88 Thermostat			25		

Improvements/Equipment

New Kitchen Cabinets 8/43

ANNUAL Expenses: _____

Taxes: (R.E.) _____ 6,116

_____ 324

Insurance: _____

Water & Sewer Tax   168

© 1989 Michal E. Feder

RENTAL *is a summary to use in preparing tax returns. Although the federal tax form lists 13 categories of expenses on rental properties, you do not need to report each separately. To maintain simplicity, expenses are grouped logically.* **FEES** *include commissions, legal & accounting, licenses;* **MANAGEMENT**—*repairs, supplies, replacements, janitorial, gardening, garbage;* **UTILITIES**—*water, gas, electricity, telephone.* **ANNUAL EXPENSES** *are tracked below to avoid wasting a column for one or two entries a year.* **AUTO** *is included because it's 50 miles every time I visit my rental. Depending on the distance and frequency of trips, you might want to substitute another category.*

   RENTAL *can also be used to keep a running track of expenses, adding pages as needed. Use the back of the page to note date and amount of income received.*

Year _____ Location _____ ► *RENTAL*

Gross Income:_____% of Ownership:_____ Net Income:_____

EXPENSES:	Fees	Mortgage (Interest)	Maintenance	Utilities	Auto (Travel)

Improvements/Equipment

_____

_____

_____

ANNUAL Expenses: _____

Taxes: _____

Insurance: _____

► **INSURANCE COVERAGE—SUMMARY**

Prepared _10/88_

Type	Company/Agent	Policy No.	Amount	Premium	Due
Life (1)	Mid At. Mutual / Jones	XXX00	100,000	969	7/88
Life (2)	Big Chief / self	XOOXX	50,000	215	8/88
Annuity (2)	Fair Play / Brown	1122XX0	15,454	none	
Annuity (2)	" "	1211XX0	8,745	none	
			Included in homeowner's fees		
Home			contents 32,000	171	5/88
Homeowner's	OK Ins. / Smith	HOXX110	annual 1,692	141 monthly	
Medical	HMO / none	1212 11X (2ears)		1,395	4/88
Car	OK Ins. / Smith	211X000		80	
Accident	Worldwide / ?		10,000	121	
Accident	U.S. Express		25,000	Included with card	
Accident	Miss card				

Notes/Reminders _Get numbers for accident policies!_

7/84 Included coverage for Macintosh

1/85 Added earthquake coverage to homeowner's
-contents - Exterior covered by Homeowner's Assn.

(1) Spouse
(2) Self

1988 Totals 4,643 (Est.)

INSURANCE *came into being because my husband can't resist inexpensive high-reward accident policies. I decided it might help to know what he had, with whom, and how to follow up in the unlikely event that I needed to follow up. Once started, it seemed to make sense to have all the key data about our insurance in one place. The added payoff for me has been getting and keeping a clear handle on just how much we are spending for protection each year, especially as a percentage of our total income. You can also use it to monitor and update your personal property insurance, a form of coverage that is easy to forget.*

► *INSURANCE COVERAGE—SUMMARY*

Type	Company/Agent	Policy No.	Amount	Premium Due

Notes/Reminders _____

_____

_____

_____

	19__85__	19__86__	19__87__
1. Wages/Salaries	25,745	23,400	17,035
2. Business Income	18,040	19,200	21,365
3. Total Income	43,650	45,455	54,345
4. Interest/Dividends	5,970	2,110	4,600
5. Capital Gains	6,365	5,530	12,800*
6. Contributions: IRA	3,000	4,000	2,000
IRA-Non-Ded			2,000
Keogh		2,880	3,220
7. Adjusted Gross	39,470	36,175	46,775
8. Taxable Income	34,350	27,780	43,200
9. Total Tax	11,238	8,654	14,760
10. Tax Bracket	State 9% Federal 37%	5% 29%	9% 35%
11. Actual (by %)	25.7%	19%	27%

Notes/Reminders ___contributions___ 1250 1398

Track expenses more carefully, pre-pay more in December? * Plan ahead for limited Partnership distributions!

This form tracks critical tax information that a financial planner or tax preparer will want to know before advising you. 1 through 9 are from the first two pages of your tax return. Tax brackets can be found listed as "marginal" tax rate on the tax rate schedules; actual % you calculate for yourself.

You can photocopy the first two pages of each year's return and put that in your notebook instead. I prefer to have the key information on one page clearly summarizing how I'm doing. I use the "Notes" section to track contributions or anything else I want to follow from year to year.

	19___	19___	19___
1. Wages/Salaries			
2. Business Income			
3. Total Income			
4. Interest/Dividends			
5. Capital Gains			
6. Contributions: IRA			
IRA-Non-Ded			
Keogh			
7. Adjusted Gross			
8. Taxable Income			
9. Total Tax			
10. Tax Bracket			
11. Actual (by %)			

Notes/Reminders _____

_____

_____

_____

_____

_____

Prepared **6/88** Tax Year **1987**

Form (Schedule and/or No)	Old / New	Total
1040		
Schedule A. — Itemized Ded.	✓	
Schedule B — Int/Div Inc.	✓	
Schedule C — Business P/L	✓	
Schedule D — Cap. Gains/Losses	✓	
Schedule E — Rents/Royalties	✓	<616>
4797 — Sales/Exchanges	✓	
6251 — Alt. Min. Tax	✓	
8271 — Tax Shelter Reg.	✓	
8606 — Non-Ded. IRA	✓	2,000
8582 — Passive Activities	✓	

Notes _Request for extension filed 4/10; returns filed 6/22. Overpaid. Reduce pre-payment for next year._
→ Remember to track non-deductible IRA (line 13) each year.

Several years ago I learned the hard way that even though I was paying a professional, to prepare our tax returns I had to know enough to be able to review them intelligently. So the first reason for including the **CHECKLIST** *in your notebook is to verify that your current return includes all the necessary forms. Start by listing every form included in last year's return. Use it when reviewing this year's return before signing it.*

An equally important reason is to check and highlight what kinds of records you need to be keeping for each schedule and be sure you have an adequate system for doing so. A major premise of this system is that it is much easier, less time-consuming, and less frustrating to record as you go along, than to reconstruct.

Form (Schedule and/or No)	Old / New	Total

Notes _____

_____

_____

_____

►*RECORDS ANALYSIS FORMS*

Prepared __6/88__ Owner _____

	Cost/ Purchase Date	Value (E)	Equity	Risk	Tax Benefits	%
Real Estate:	177,865 5/85	191,000	51,000	LOW	✓	13
Personal	262,000 12/87	288,000	33,600 *	Medium	✓	8.6
Investment						
Cash Equiv.:			1,500	low		
Checking			15,430	low		
Savings						
CDs						
Securities:			68,470	med. to low	cap gains only	17.5
Stocks			48,601	low		12.4
Bonds					188	
Partnerships:			65,000 (E)	Med-Hi	-8,672	
Real Estate	58,000					
Oil & Gas	10,000		10,000	Hi		
Other						
Insurance:						
Life						
(cash value)			23,432	low		
Annuities	10,000				✓ 188	
Retirement:			21,021	medium	2000	
IRA	11,044		26,639	Medium		
Keogh	21,000					
Pension						
Other:			10,000 ①	low		
Gold/Silver			15,000	low		
Collectibles						
Grand Totals			389,693			

75

© 1989 Michal E. Feder

* 40% equity
① Community property

The basic idea of asset allocation is to reduce risk by diversifying assets. Major categories are listed. For anything purchased over time, such as a home, subtract the mortgage balance to arrive at your current equity. Retirement accounts are separated because they are a special reserve being set aside for the future. You can use the blank columns for analysis choosing risk, liquidity, expected rate of return, time frame, tax benefits, etc. You can skip all or part of the Cost column. (It's a way to keep in mind where you started and where you are now.) Divide each category's total into the Grand Total to find the percent of your total assets it represents.

*　　**ASSET ALLOCATION** gives you a way to evaluate the information you collected in creating a **NET WORTH** statement (pp. 29, 31). You can create your own asset allocation form as you did for **WORKSHEET** (p. 27).*

	Cost/ Purchase Date	Value (E)	Equity	Risk	Tax Benefits	%
Real Estate:						
Personal						
Investment						
Cash Equiv.:						
Checking						
Savings						
CDs						
Securities:						
Stocks						
Bonds						
Partnerships:						
Real Estate						
Oil & Gas						
Other						
Insurance:						
Life						
(cash value)						
Annuities						
Retirement:						
IRA						
Keogh						
Pension						
Other:						
Gold/Silver						
Collectibles						
Grand Totals						

19 **88**

Name	Shares	Invested To Date	Additions	Reinvested	Shares	Total Cost	Basis per sh.
R.E. Fund	1,114	11,752		1,577	1,273	13,329	
Global II	429	6,714	1,000	507	517	8,221	15.90
Marvelous Mutual	819	5,048		638	903	5,686	6.29
Lovely Lighting	127	6,096	4,800	424	171	8,320	48.65

Notes _Return on R.E. Fund 13.45 for year — partly tax sheltered — continue to reinvest next year?_

Financial professionals are amazed at the number of people who pay higher profit taxes or claim smaller losses than they are entitled to because they don't keep adequate records of their reinvestments in stocks, funds, REITS, etc. You can update **COST BASIS** *in pencil when you receive notice of a distribution if you are thinking of selling; otherwise, once a year.*

Use this form and your stock or fund cumulative year-end statement for tax purposes. To calculate your basis (current cost per share), divide the total cost by total number of shares currently owned. Reconstructing the record for prior years might not be worth it, but that shouldn't stop you from doing better in the future.

Kept current, this form can be invaluable if you want to quickly estimate the profit or loss and tax consequences of selling any of your investments.

Name	Shares	Invested To Date	Additions	Reinvested	Shares	Total Cost	Basis per sh.

Notes _____

_____

_____

_____

Prepared **9/87**

	No. of Shares	$ Value	Price per Share
Current:	773	$35,940	46.49
Starting:* (1/1/87)	753	28,064	37.26

$ Profit : **7,876**

% Profit : **28**

Acceptable Stop–%: **18**

Starting Value = **$ 28,064**

18 % of S.V. = **5052**

Acceptable $ = **33,116** ÷ **773** = **$42.84**
Current Shares   P.P.S

---

* *Starting Point* is optional—beginning of investment, since last switch, since beginning of year, etc.

% Profit is calculated by dividing *$ Profit* into *Starting Profit.*

Acceptable Stop is discretionary depending on the comfort zone of the investor, the volatility of the investment, it's history, etc.

Acceptable $ is found by multiplying the Acceptable % by the Starting $. This figure added to the Starting $ gives you the $ amount you want to preserve. Dividing that by your current number of shares gives the price per share at which you need to sell to protect the % gain you established with your choice of an Acceptable Stop. This does not include tax consequences of selling. Long-term investors probably should update the cost basis and estimate the tax they will have to pay based on last year's tax bracket (combined—state and federal) and factor that into their decision.

Tax Consequences: sell @ 42.84 → 33,116
cost basis → 18,045
Profit → 15,071
taxes (37%) 5,576

33,116
− 5,576
$27,540 (Net)

CREATING A STOP *was born during the summer of 1987 as stocks moved ever higher and some of the experts began talking about caution, discipline, and preserving capital. As a long-term investor rather than a trader, I looked for a way to focus on what I wanted to gain rather than what I was willing to lose.*

I created hypothetical stops for a limited number of my most volatile investments that had made the biggest gains in recent months. I arrived at an acceptable stop for each by broadly figuring the profits that I wanted to preserve. Obviously the time to create stops is as the market moves up.

In this example, my investment had advanced $7867 (28%) during 1987. To preserve the 18% gain I selected, I would have to sell when the price per share declined to $42.84.

	No. of Shares	$ Value	Price per Share
Current:	_____	_____	_____
Starting:*	_____	_____	_____

$ **Profit** : _____

% **Profit** : _____

Acceptable Stop – %: _____

Starting Value = _____

___**% of S.V.** = _____

Acceptable $ = _____ ÷ _____ = _____

Current Shares   P.P.S

* *Starting Point* is optional—beginning of investment, since last switch, since beginning of year, etc.

% Profit is calculated by dividing *$ Profit* into *Starting Profit.*

Acceptable Stop is discretionary depending on the comfort zone of the investor, the volatility of the investment, it's history, etc.

Acceptable $ is found by multiplying the Acceptable % by the Starting $. This figure added to the Starting $ gives you the $ amount you want to preserve. Dividing that by your current number of shares gives the price per share at which you need to sell to protect the % gain you established with your choice of an Acceptable Stop. This does not include tax consequences of selling. Long-term investors probably should update the cost basis and estimate the tax they will have to pay based on last year's tax bracket (combined—state and federal) and factor that into their decision.

Prepared __1988__

Purchase Price
170,000

Down Payment
34,000

Mortgage/Rate
136,000 / 9.5%

1 How much do I currently have invested in my home?

$$220,000 \quad 132,000 = 88,000$$

Current Value (E) – Mortgage Balance = Current Equity

2 How much has my home appreciated?

$$220,000 - 170,000 = 50,000 / 29.41\%$$

Current Value (E) – Purchase Price = $ amount / %

3 What is my return on invested $?

$$34,000 \qquad 88,000 \qquad 38.63\%$$

Down payment ÷ Current Equity

4 What has been the annualized rate of return?

$$38.6\% \div 4 = 9.6\%$$

% divided by years owned

5 How much do I expect it to appreciate over the next 1–3 years?

15 %

$$.15 \times 220,000 = +33,000$$

6 Tax Benefits:

Tax deduction for interest on mortgage

| 12,240 | 4,529 |
| Amount | Est Tax Savings |

Tax deduction for real estate taxes

| 1,940 | 718 |
| Amount | Est Tax Savings |

Homeowner's exemption

| 7,000 | 72 |
| Amount | Est Tax Savings |

7 What major expenses can I anticipate during the next three years?

Retile Bath / 1,000 + new Deck / 1500 + Item/Amount

Item/Amount   Item/Amount   Item/Amount

_____ + _____ + _____ + =

Item/Amount   Item/Amount   Item/Amount   Total

8 Notes

© 1989 Michal E. Feder

Most planners I have talked with want to exclude an owner-occupied residence from any discussion or financial plan. I think that omission ignores a very important reality since, for most people, their home is their major asset. Some people will sell and move to larger or smaller homes several times. Home equity loans, reverse mortgages, and sales to children with lifetime occupancy guaranteed are being used increasingly to extract dollars from homes for present use. So keeping the record (See p. 61) and evaluating the record periodically makes sense.

This form does not provide an exact financial analysis, but it does present the broad picture. Current Value on Line 1 can be your educated guess or that of a realtor. Percent on Line 2 is found by dividing the appreciation ($ amount) by the purchase price.

Purchase Price	Down Payment	Mortgage/Rate

1 How much do I currently have invested in my home?

_____

Current Value (E) – Mortgage Balance = Current Equity

2 How much has my home appreciated?

_____

Current Value (E) – Purchase Price = $ amount / %

3 What is my return on invested $? _____

Down payment ÷ Current Equity

4 What has been the annualized rate of return? _____

% divided by years owned

5 How much do I expect it to appreciate over the next 1–3 years? ____%

6 Tax Benefits:

Tax deduction for interest on mortgage

_____

Amount   Est Tax Savings

Tax deduction for real estate taxes

_____

Amount   Est Tax Savings

Homeowner's exemption

_____

Amount   Est Tax Savings

7 What major expenses can I anticipate during the next three years?

_____

Item/Amount   +   Item/Amount   +   Item/Amount

_____

Item/Amount   +   Item/Amount   +   Item/Amount   =   Total

8 Notes _____

_____

_____

_____

_____

Source	Date	Earned Self	Earned Spouse	Portfolio Int.	Portfolio Div	Passive Payout	Passive Other
Prepared _1988_ Year/Month _Jan._							
Social Security	1/3		960				
Self Emp.	1/8	510					
"	1/12		200				
"	1/14	225					
R. & Co.	1/15			371			
Lucky Leasing	1/21					580	
R.E. Fund	1/22				280		
Sale of old car	1/25						500*

Notes * sold for 2,200 — Balance due in three payments by 6/1

© 1989 Michal E. Feder

INCOME SUMMARY became a double-purpose form when the Tax Reform Act of 1986 created three categories of income. Originally I designed it to track income during the transition period into retirement as earned income decreased and the need for investment earnings increased. Adding a line dividing income into earned, portfolio, or passive categories makes it possible to monitor for adjusting estimated tax payments, earned income for Social Security retirees, and month to month variations in **MONEY IN** (See p. 21). This form is a way of looking at the information as an investor/tax-payer rather than a budgeter.

I try to prepay what I expect to owe but no more. Remember, the government does not pay interest on the excess you prepay until after your return is reviewed which may be six weeks after you file it, and then only if the refund is delayed.

Source	Date	Earned		Portfolio		Passive	
		Self	Spouse	Int.	Div	Payout	Other

Notes _____

_____

_____

_____

_____

INVESTMENT RECORD

Year __1988__   Owner __Independent Investor__ ► INVESTMENT RECORD

Name	Date	New	Reinvest	Amount
Excellent Oil	1/10	5,000	755	Oil
First Fund	1/15		891	M.M.
Excellent Equity Fd.	2/3	4,000		Stock
Global II	4/6	4,000	507	Int'l
Marvelous Mutual	4/15		638	Stock
Lovely Lighting	6/12	1,800	424	Util.
R.E. Fund	6/30		1,577	R.E.

Questions:

How much have I invested this year? __$8,800 (new)__

How much have I reinvested/added to prior investments? __4,792__

TOTALS: __13,592__

Notes for next year __Try to increase totals to $20,000 next year. Avoid new investments Add to best of existing ones.__

The questions at the bottom of the page are what led to the creation of this form. When you put aside dollars to invest you often must choose whether to add to investments you already have or venture into something new. Sticking with what you have is usually easier, and certainly involves less record-keeping, but some investments complete their cycle and then might be the time to move on.

I used **INVESTMENT RECORD** several years ago to monitor a shift to more energy related assets, as recommended by an investment advisor. I also have used it in moving between investments in the same sector as shown on this example.

If you have this form ready to go, it takes almost no time to construct from year end cumulative statements that arrive during January and February each year.

Name	Date	New	Reinvest	Amount

Questions:

How much have I invested this year? _____

How much have I reinvested/added to prior investments?_____

TOTALS: _____

Notes for next year _____

_____

_____

Year __1988__ Owner __Self__

Name	Invested to Date	Additions	Value 3/31	Value 6/31	Value 9/30	Value 12/31
New Fund	4,259	2,000	6,350	6,666	7,112	10,015
Far East Fd.	2,000		2,550	2,815	3,038	3,081
Mid West Fd.	7,186		9,361	9,848	10,634	11,078
Healthcare	1,727		1,780	2,286	2,807	2,634 *

Notes __* Moved to money market 11/18__

Some people enjoy checking out the stock pages every day and others never look. I wanted the simplest possible way to track key information. I wanted to verify how I was doing, what to watch, and when to sell or add to existing investments. My version is set up as an annual form and I update it quarterly.

Three key pieces of information are easy to spot if you use this form: Your current profit in any particular stock or fund, the relationship between investment and profit among different items, and how much money you have added to your portfolio this year. Finally, collecting this information in summary form makes it a matter of a few calculations and a few minutes to check your results against the experts, the market, or any criteria you have set for yourself.

Year _____ Owner _____   ▶ *INVESTMENT UPDATE*

Name	Invested to Date	Additions	Value	Value	Value	Value

Notes _____

_____

_____

_____

Tax Year _1988 (year end)_

Name	Date	Stocks %/Amt	Bonds %/Amt	Cash Equivalents %/Amt
Midwest		79/8751	8/886	13/1440
New Fund		80/7558	3/283	18/1200
Old Glory		72/25,021	7/2432	21/7287
		41,330	3,601	10,430

Bond Portfolio		+45,000	
		$ 48,601	

Other stocks	25,000	
" " Funds	2,140	
	68,470	

Notes _year end totals:_

Stocks	68,470
Bonds	48,601
Cash Equiv.	10,430 *

* plus savings accts. + money market accts.

Most financial experts encourage you to strike a balance among stocks, bonds, and cash equivalents or money market accounts. Your balance is easy to figure if you own individual stocks or bonds, but many mutual funds have mixtures. I developed this form to clarify how aggressive/defensive my fund portfolio really was.

The allocations are presented in percentages in quarterly and annual reports (not the fund prospectus). Each fund will probably represent a different proportion of your total portfolio, so you will have to make some calculations. Multiply the % listed in the most recent report by the current total $ value (shares owned × current price) in the fund to get the $ amount in each category. Add the column and divide it into the combined current value of all your funds. This will not be perfect, but it can produce useful information when you need it.

Name	Date	Stocks %/Amt	Bonds %/Amt	Cash Equivalents %/Amt

Notes _____

_____

_____

_____

Year __1988__ Description __Big City Flat__   ▶ REAL ESTATE

Ownership/% __self / 40%__

Purchase Date __12/15/87__

Use __Rental__

Total Cost __262,000__

Mortgage/Rate __205,000__   __8.125%__

$ Invested __23,290__

Loan No. __XXOOXOXO__

Gross Income __7620__

– Operating Expenses __3445__   (40% of total)

Net Operating Income __4175__

– Interest on loan __6624__

Net Income/Loss __< 2449 >__

– Depreciation   __3205__
(see tax preparer)

Taxable Income/(Loss)   __< 5654 >__

Evaluation:

Taxable Income/Loss   __< 5654 >__

– Tax Savings   __2092__
(Taxable Income/loss
x combined tax bracket) __3562__
Net Gain/(Loss)

288,000 Est. value
204,000 Current Mort.
─────────
84,000
↓
33,600 (40%)

Current Return on   __< – 15% >__
Invested $
gain/loss ÷ Invested $
Current Value (E)   __288,000__

Current Equity (E)   33,600
– Total Cost to Date   26,853
(Invested $ + or –   ─────────
net gains or losses)
Current Profit on $ 6,747
invested $

Notes/Reminders _____

© 1989 Michal E. Feder

REAL ESTATE combines a baseline record with a simplified profit and loss statement and an evaluation of the property as an investment; in other words, where you started, what it's costing or earning for you, and what the projected profit is so far. Because real estate is primarily a long-term investment, it will become more valuable after several years, when you begin to see cumulative benefits in taxes saved and increased equity as you pay the mortgage and the property appreciates. Conversely, gathering these numbers all in one place in an orderly fashion might help you to realize it's time to take your losses and move on.

This form works particularly well for owners of one or two investment properties, or a second home that is also income property.

Year _____ Description _____   ► *REAL ESTATE*

Ownership/%   Purchase Date   Use

Total Cost
$ Invested   Mortgage/Rate
         Loan No.

Gross Income

    – Operating Expenses

Net Operating Income

    – Interest on loan

Net Income/Loss

    – Depreciation

Taxable Income/Loss

Evaluation:

Taxable Income/Loss

    – Tax Savings

        Net Gain/Loss

Current Return on
Invested $

Current Value (E)   Current Equity (E)
        – Total Cost to Date

        Current Profit on
        invested $

Notes/Reminders _____

►*READY REFERENCE*

INVESTMENT INFORMATION

As soon as you start to invest in a stock, a fund, or a limited partnership, you initiate an avalanche of information. Some of it has current or temporary value. Some can serve as reference points for future tracking or evaluating. Over the years, I have found the following to be the information I refer back to and really use:

- ☐ Year-end summaries of all distributions and additions to funds, stock reinvestment programs, partnerships (discard interim notices at year end).

- ☐ 1099 forms used in preparing taxes.

- ☐ Projections of tax consequences sent by partnerships and funds (discard when 1099s arrive in Jan.–Mar.).

- ☐ Current prospectus for each fund, bank account, etc.

- ☐ Latest annual report for each fund, stock (discard quarterly and other reports unless unusual information).

- ☐ Special annual summaries. Examples: *Forbes*—August review of mutual funds and January review of American industry, *Fortune* and *Inc.* magazine annual reviews.

Please note—I am referring to *information*—not the documents/records you need to keep for tax and legal purposes.

RECORDS

Proof of ownership: deeds, titles, brokerage, valuables.
Proof of entitlement: insurance policies, warranties, contracts, inherited goods and property, copies of estate and gift tax returns if possible.
Tax-related checks: (stubs are not sufficient) for all deductions such as medical, business-related, taxes, charitable contributions, investment related expenses, home improvements. Keep K-1's and 1099's for the life of each investment.
Bills/Receipts that substantiate these where appropriate. Example: Bills that show prescription drugs, donations of goods to charities, finance charges.
Buy and Sell records for all purchases that have tax consequences.

Tax documentation records should be kept for *at least three years*—more if you are using any complex tax-avoidance strategies.

Proof of ownership, buy and sell records, old tax returns, home purchase and improvements—*indefinitely.*

Discard last year's bills, lapsed insurance policies, out-of-date warranties, to make room for this year's.

The first step is to separate what's essential from the rest. Then make a personal decision what you find useful. Establish specific locations for these records and start creating an inventory of what you are keeping where.

I keep:
- ☐ hard-to-replace records (birth certificates, etc.) in a safe deposit box.
- ☐ working/current records in file folders near my desk.
- ☐ wills, insurance policies, infrequently used credit cards, etc. in a metal strongbox nearby.
- ☐ current tax information (3 years) in a box, with easy access; older records in *well marked* file boxes in the closet.

TIP: The key is to *separate, discard, be consistent, and do it continuously.*

►ASSET LOCATION INVENTORY

Name _____ Date _____

Employer _____

Social Security No. _____ - _____ - _____

_____

Location of Records

    A. Residence _____
                  Address

    B. Safe Deposit Box _____
                    Number   Bank   Address

    C. Office _____
             Address

    D. _____

    E. _____

    F. _____

Location   Item*   Notes

A	B	C	D	E	F	Item	Notes
☐	☐	☐	☐	☐	☐	Annuity contracts	
☐	☐	☐	☐	☐	☐	Auto ownership records	
☐	☐	☐	☐	☐	☐	Bank statements, canceled checks	
☐	☐	☐	☐	☐	☐	Birth certificate	
☐	☐	☐	☐	☐	☐	Bonds	
☐	☐	☐	☐	☐	☐	Brokerage account records	
☐	☐	☐	☐	☐	☐	Burial instructions	
☐	☐	☐	☐	☐	☐	Car insurance policy	
☐	☐	☐	☐	☐	☐	Cemetery plot deed	
☐	☐	☐	☐	☐	☐	Certificates of deposit	
☐	☐	☐	☐	☐	☐	Checkbooks	
☐	☐	☐	☐	☐	☐	Citizenship papers	
☐	☐	☐	☐	☐	☐	Corporate retirement plan	
☐	☐	☐	☐	☐	☐	Divorce/separation records	
☐	☐	☐	☐	☐	☐	Employment contracts	
☐	☐	☐	☐	☐	☐	Health insurance policy	
☐	☐	☐	☐	☐	☐	Homeowners insurance policy	
☐	☐	☐	☐	☐	☐	Income and gift tax returns	
☐	☐	☐	☐	☐	☐	Keogh or IRA plan	
☐	☐	☐	☐	☐	☐	Life insurance	
☐	☐	☐	☐	☐	☐	Life insurance, individual	
☐	☐	☐	☐	☐	☐	List of checking and savings accounts	

* To save your family/heirs frustration, cross out all items on this list that you don't have—anywhere!

Location						Item*	Notes
A	**B**	**C**	**D**	**E**	**F**		
☐	☐	☐	☐	☐	☐	List of stored and loaned valuable possessions_____	
☐	☐	☐	☐	☐	☐	Marriage certificate_____	
☐	☐	☐	☐	☐	☐	Military discharge papers_____	
☐	☐	☐	☐	☐	☐	Mutual fund shares _____	
☐	☐	☐	☐	☐	☐	Notes and other loan agreements, including mortgates_____	
☐	☐	☐	☐	☐	☐	Other death benefits _____	
☐	☐	☐	☐	☐	☐	Other securities_____	
☐	☐	☐	☐	☐	☐	Partnership agreements _____	
☐	☐	☐	☐	☐	☐	Passports _____	
☐	☐	☐	☐	☐	☐	Powers of attorney_____	
☐	☐	☐	☐	☐	☐	Profit-sharing plan_____	
☐	☐	☐	☐	☐	☐	Property and casualty insurance_____	
☐	☐	☐	☐	☐	☐	Record of investment securities_____	
☐	☐	☐	☐	☐	☐	Rental property records_____	
☐	☐	☐	☐	☐	☐	Safe deposit box key_____	
☐	☐	☐	☐	☐	☐	Savings passbooks _____	
☐	☐	☐	☐	☐	☐	Special bequests _____	
☐	☐	☐	☐	☐	☐	Stock certificates _____	
☐	☐	☐	☐	☐	☐	Stock-option plan_____	
☐	☐	☐	☐	☐	☐	Stock-purchase plan_____	
☐	☐	☐	☐	☐	☐	Tax returns_____	
☐	☐	☐	☐	☐	☐	Title insurance_____	
☐	☐	☐	☐	☐	☐	Titles and deeds to real estate and land_____	
☐	☐	☐	☐	☐	☐	Trust agreements_____	
☐	☐	☐	☐	☐	☐	Will (copy)_____	
☐	☐	☐	☐	☐	☐	Will (original)_____	
☐	☐	☐	☐	☐	☐	_____	
☐	☐	☐	☐	☐	☐	_____	
☐	☐	☐	☐	☐	☐	_____	
☐	☐	☐	☐	☐	☐	_____	
☐	☐	☐	☐	☐	☐	_____	
☐	☐	☐	☐	☐	☐	_____	
☐	☐	☐	☐	☐	☐	_____	

Important Names, Addresses, and Phone Numbers

Accountant _____
  Name   Address

Attorney _____
  Name   Address

Financial Advisor _____
  Name   Address

Next of Kin _____
  Name   Address

Trustee _____
  Name   Address

Other _____
  Name   Address

Lent → 6/12/85 - To LAW - Shaw - Material on Consulting Ret ✓

Lent → 10/1 - J Career Consulting, Inventories - Ret ✓

Lent → 11/2/86 - TBF - Mutual Fund Guide ('86)

    - Video & Directions Ret 12/20

    - Life Insurance Folders

    2/87 - Business License - In Personal Papers (Red File)

MASTER INDEX [C]

8/80 Computer Articles - Separate File

    Bottom Drawer / Personal

2/83 Copyright correspondence - Green folder

    with Franchise Tax Info.

MASTER INDEX [S]

2/83 Sam Small - Personal Note in safe deposit box

    Subscriptions - New file 1/85 - Red in Personal

    Speeches - Separate file in closet

    List with P/R Folder

11/86 Symphony. Acct. no & correspondence in

    Personal file

Notes Social Security nos. - family list including

    grandchildren - in Money Map Ref. section

© 1989 Michal E. Feder

Do you ever wonder where to put things, or where they are now? The basic premise of **MASTER INDEX** is to track your actions, not judge them, and remove the necessity of remembering where you put things you tend to misplace.

Make 26 copies of this form and label them A-Z. The next time you puzzle over where to put something, record it under the appropriate letter. Be sure to date your entry and cross off items as they become out of date. By adding another 30 seconds to the process of putting something someplace, you can give up forever worrying about losing it.

Warning: Papers that you abandon in process and shove into a pile to deal with later are the worst offenders. It's OK to quit. Just leave a marker.

Notes _____

Prepared _January_   Year _1988_

Month	Item	Amount	Notes
Jan.	IRA/first pay.	1,000	First
	Lakeside	900	Inst. family share
Feb.	Home Improve Re-tile shower	4,000 (E)	8,000 total 4,000 loan
Mar.	New car	2,000	
April	Property taxes	750	ck. with tax preparer Try not to overpay!
	Fed/state taxes		
May	Car Insurance	698	
	Home owner's Ins.	171	?
June	Fed/state taxes		
July	Life Insurance	969	
Aug.	Vacation	1,200	Trip to Lakeside
	Life Insurance	215	
Sept.	Lakeside	900	Second Inst. family sh. ?
	Fed/state taxes		
Oct.			
Nov.	Car Insurance	698	
Dec.	Property taxes	750	?
	Fed/state taxes		

Notes _____

_____

_____

_____

EXPENSE CALENDAR developed because I find it more comfortable to space major expenses throughout the year. It can also help those on a tight budget to anticipate and possibly control the overuse of credit cards. Year to year, it's a quick way to track without going through the process on pp. 21, 23. Thus, you can use it to plan or predict.

With different items coming due throughout the year I am more apt to give each some attention. This year, I reviewed our car insurance and decided to stay with our present coverage. Last year, I reviewed our homeowners insurance and decided to switch. Some major items to consider are income taxes, property taxes, all insurance, a new car, necessary purchases or replacements of major appliances, elective surgery, a special trip.

Month	Item	Amount	Notes

Notes _____

Prepared _1988_	Owner _Joan_			
Item	Location	Record	Appraisal	Notes
Mom's Pearls	Safe Dep.			Save for L. ?
Emerald Earrings	"			For B.
Silver Service	at home	Home Safe	✓	
Duck Sculpture	"	✓	2,500	Add for copy
"Star" Sculpture	"		2/83 2,300	Loaned to T 4/88
Video Camera	"		3/84 3,000	
Computer	"		→get one!	For T?
Garden Statue				

Notes _Make separate list of household items (furniture especially) before next insurance premium. Figure out how to establish value on paintings_

There are a number of good reasons to record and track **PERSONAL PROPERTY**. It is valuable for insurance purposes. It is part of any net worth statement. Many items increase/decrease in value over time and most people accumulate/divest at various stages of their lives. **NET WORTH** (p. 31) gives you the snapshot view. **PERSONAL PROPERTY** shows how you arrived at your totals and adds the dimension of change over time.

I use the **NOTES** column a lot on this particular form to remind myself of decisions or steps to be taken and inform others of my wishes. If an item has a high dollar or sentimental value, it's probably worth adding as an addendum to your will as well.

Item	Location	Record	Appraisal	Notes

Notes _____

_____

_____

_____

Prepared ~~started~~ *1988*

LOCATION: *TOWN BANK*

BOX NUMBER *66*

REGISTRATION: *Self and Spouse*

Document/Item	Original	Duplicate	Deposited	Removed
Birth Certificates	✓	✓	3/88	2/88 ②
Social Security Cards	✓	✓	3/85	3/85 ①
Grant Deed – Memory Lane	✓		2/82	
Title Insurance		✓	2/82	
City Savings Fund	✓	✓ at home		
Valley Bank Certif.			2/82	
Wills		✓	2/82	
Jewelry: Pearls	✓		2/82	
Earrings	✓		2/82	
New Fund	✓	✓ at home 4/86		

Notes ① *Removed to make copies for employment records for state*
② *Removed to apply for Social Security*

Safe deposit boxes are an inexpensive way to protect vital, hard to replace papers and valuables. I'm surprised how many people never bother to rent one. If you have a box and rarely change the contents, a single worksheet following your **ASSET LOCATION INVENTORY** *(p. 97), or under S if you create a* **MASTER INDEX**, *will be enough. If you do a bit of shuffling in and out like I do, you've probably found it's easy to lose sight of what's where. Setting up and maintaining this form will simplify keeping track. Be sure to update it the day you go to your box even if you only move things to another storage place in your house, or you'll be right back where you started from!*

► *SAFE DEPOSIT BOX*

LOCATION: _____ **BOX NUMBER** ____

REGISTRATION: _____

Document/Item	Original	Duplicate	Deposited	Removed

Notes _____

_____

_____

_____

Prepared 3/88

Name	Card Number	Expires	Emergency Call No.
BANK CARD	XXX-0000-XXXX	1/88	000-XXXX
Viva	0000-1111-XXXX	2/88	XXX-0000
Gold Card	1111-2222-3333	4/88	222-1212
Dept. Store	XOX-OXO-00	—	101-XOXO
Dept. Store	X 000 XXO XOX	—	020-XXOO
Gas Card	ZZZ XXX ZXZO	6/88	
Car Club	XOX ZOXZ	7/88	020-ZZXX
Medical Plan	XXOXXXO		001 2212
Library I.D.	X 000 XOXOXO1O	—	010-XZOZ
Symphony I.D.	ZOXXZZ	through May '89	030-2221
Video Club	ZO221	10/88	020-XX11

Notes Business I.D. XOX1212XO

Telephone Acct. No. Z122XX311   020-3312

→ Create Separate Business list starting in '89

I developed the **CREDIT CARDS** *form because I wanted a handy place to keep all the emergency numbers to call if my credit cards were lost or stolen. I am uncomfortable having all my cards listed in some public computer. It quickly expanded to include a lot of other identifying numbers. Some I use frequently and others seldom, but I really like having them all in one place. If you use this form begin with Bank Cards, Department Stores, Gas, Travel, Medical Plan and add any number you have to search for the next time you need it. An alternative is to list numbers as you renew or add new ones.*

Name	Card Number	Expires	Emergency Call No.

Notes _____

Year _1988-89_

☐ SUBSCRIPTIONS
☐ RENEWALS
☐ ASSOCIATIONS

Name	Renewed	Expires	Cost/Source
Post St. Journal	1/20/88	2/1/89	101 ① T
Executive	11/28/8	12/8	29 Visa T
$ $ and Sense	4/87	5/88	25 Visa T
Fund Guide	9/4/87	12/88	79 ② T Expo special
Computerease	5/1/87	8/88	15 ② T
Sports world	4/12/87	7/1/88	30 ①
KETV	3/88	3/89	50 ① T (35)
College Club	10/87	10/88	15 ②
Everyone's Political Caucus	4/87	4/88	30 ②
Symphony Assoc.	6/87	6/88	35 ① T

Notes: _( ) = amounts that are contributions —_
(tax deductable)

Like the **CREDIT CARDS** form, this one saves time and energy digging through file folders. It also alerts you to double billing particularly for subscriptions and renewals in organizations that also raise funds. I included "Expires" so I would be sure when I really needed to renew since the codes on the magazines aren't always decipherable. I added "Source" so I could quickly verify payment by check date and number if necessary. Incidentally, I have all my bank accounts coded by number to save time and space (see above). I have found that when a form really works, you quickly find other uses for it. With this one, I mark all items that can be claimed as tax deductions with a "T"—a handy reminder at tax time.

☐ **SUBSCRIPTIONS**
☐ **RENEWALS**
☐ **ASSOCIATIONS**

Name	Renewed	Expires	Cost/Source

Notes: _____

_____

_____

In keeping records as simple as possible, it's helpful to notice anything you do that's repetitive. This redemption letter is a good example. I originally designed it when I was about to leave on a long vacation and realized that a number of mutual funds I owned required a signature guarantee should I decide to sell any shares.

I didn't plan on selling but it gave me psychological insurance to leave prepared. I took my letters on vacation, brought them back and have had them on file ever since. I've only used one so far.

The letter took ten minutes to compose. It was another 20 minutes getting copies and filling them in. I spent ten minutes at the bank having all of them guaranteed at the same time—a half hour well spent.

When redeeming mutual fund shares, you can request dollar amounts or specific numbers of shares. Dollar amounts make for easier book-keeping. I set my letter up to work either way. Don't forget to photocopy a redemption letter before you send it.

_____

_____

_____

Date: _____

_____

_____

_____

_____

Re: Account _____ in the name of _____

Dear Sirs:

Please redeem _____ shares held in my account and send proceeds to me at the address above.

My Social Security No is _____. Please direct all correspondence to me at my residence:

PHONE NO _____

I am providing a signature guarantee below

Sincerely,

_____

There are a number of relatively simple ways to measure and compare expenses, investments, tax benefits, and other financial data. Here are a few that are useful for occasional reference.

The Rule of 72

Take any rate of return and divide it into 72 and you will learn how long it will take your money to double in value.

Example: $72 \div .07 = 10.2$
$72 \div .12 = 6$

$10,000 invested will take 10.2 years to double @ 7% and 6 years @ 12%.

The Rule of 144:

Adds another dimension. Given a certain annual investment, it tells you when your total investment will have doubled. Divide the rate of return into 144.

Example: $144 \div .07 = 20.6$
$144 \div .12 = 12$

Investing $1,000 each year, your total cumulative investment will double in 20.6 years @ 7% and 12 years @ 12%

Taxable vs Nontaxable:

This shows what you will have to earn in a taxable investment to equal a nontaxable one. Subtract your marginal tax rate (combined federal and state tax bracket) from 1.0. Divide that into the projected yield on any investment.

Example: $1.0 - .37$ (combined tax bracket) $= .63$
$.07 \div .63 = .11$
$.12 \div .63 = .19$

If you are in the 37% tax bracket you will need a taxable investment of 11.1% to equal a nontaxable one earning 7%, or 19% to equal one earning 12%.

Capital to Income:

To quickly calculate how much capital you will need to provide a specific income, divide the income wanted by the assumed rate of return.

Example: Income desired is $40.000. Rate of return
is 7% or $30,000 @ 12%
$40,000 \div .07 = $571,428$
$30,000 \div .12 = $250,000$

The Magic of Compounding:

Even if you only invest a lump sum once, it's impressive to see how it will grow if you leave it alone. Notice how the rate of appreciation accelerates especially after ten years or more.

Here's what would happen to a $10,000 investment.
Years Invested at

Year	5%	6%	7%	8%	9%	10%	11%	12%
1	$ 10,500	$ 10,600	$ 10,700	$ 10,800	$ 10,900	$11,000	$ 11,100	$ 11,200
2	11,025	11,236	11,449	11,664	11,881	12,100	12,321	11,544
3	11,576	11,910	12,250	12,597	12,950	13,310	13,676	14,049
4	12,155	12,625	13,108	13,605	14,116	14,641	15,181	15,735
5	12,763	13,382	14,026	14,693	15,386	16,105	16,851	17,623
6	13,401	14,185	15,007	15,869	16,771	17,716	18,704	19,738
7	14,071	15,036	16,058	17,138	18,280	19,487	20,762	22,107
8	14,775	15,938	17,182	18,509	19,926	21,436	23,046	24,760
9	15,513	16,895	18,385	19,990	21,719	23,579	25,580	27,731
10	16,289	17,908	19,672	21,589	23,674	25,937	28,394	31,058
11	17,103	18,983	21,049	23,316	25,804	28,531	31,518	34,785
12	17,959	20,122	22,522	25,182	28,127	31,384	34,984	38.960
13	18,856	21,329	24,098	27,196	30,658	34,523	38,833	43,635
14	19,799	22,609	25,785	29,372	33,417	37,974	43,104	48,871
15	20,789	23,966	27,590	31,722	36,425	41,772	47,846	54,736
16	21,829	25,404	29,522	34,259	39,703	45,950	53,109	61,304
17	22,920	26,928	31,589	37,000	43,276	50,545	58,951	68,660
18	24,066	28,543	33,799	39,960	47,171	55,599	65,436	76,900
19	25,270	30,256	36,165	43,157	51,416	61,159	72,633	86,128
20	26,533	32,071	38,697	46,609	56,044	67,274	80,623	96,463
21	27,860	33,996	41,406	50,338	61,088	74,002	89,492	108,038
22	29,253	36,035	44,304	54,365	66,586	81,403	99,336	121,003
23	30,715	38,197	47,405	58,714	72,579	89,543	110,263	135,523
24	32,251	40,489	50,724	63,412	79,111	98,497	122,392	151,786
25	33,864	42,919	54,274	68,484	86,231	108,347	135,855	170,001

How Long Will It Last?

Most people will have to or want to supplement their basic retirement benefits, such as pension plans and Social Security. Entrepreneurs and independent professionals who have not been able to contribute enough to self-created plans will also face this question. For many years, I asked a variety of professionals for a simple formula to calculate how much of an asset base I would need to assure the life-style I wanted during my retirement years.

The tables below are the closest I have come. They project as far out as 30 years. That is, blank entries mean you can withdraw the desired amount for at least 30 years.

1. Begin by adding up the annual income you will be receiving from all other sources such as pensions, social security, and other retirement plans.
2. Determine or estimate your total invested capital exclusive of your home and pension plans (company plans, IRAs, and Keoghs).
3. Decide how many dollars you will want each year *in addition to* your pension and other retirement benefits.
4. Figure that amount (Step 3) as a percentage of your estimated invested capital (Step 2).
5. Pick one of the tables below with the withdrawal rate closest to your estimate.
6. Decide on an earnings rate you believe is reasonable and an average inflation rate you wish to allow for.
7. The tables will show how many years on an inflation-adjusted basis your capital will last.

NOTE: These figures might look different from others you have seen. Many tables allow for withdrawing a constant % so as your capital decreases you will be withdrawing fewer actual dollars. Also, most that I have seen assume 0% inflation.

TABLE 1 If each year you withdraw an inflation-adjusted amount equal to 5% of your initial invested capital,

And inflation is: While your total return on the remaining amount is →

And inflation is	3%	6%	9%	12%	15%	18%	21%
0%	30	-	-	-	-	-	-
2%	23						
4%	19	25					
6%	16	20	29				
8%	15	18	22				
10%	14	16	19	25			
12%	13	14	17	20	28		
14%	12	13	15	18	22		

TABLE 2 If you withdraw an inflation adjusted-amount equal to 10% of your original invested capital each year, the numbers will look like this:

Inflation	Total return on balance →						
	3%	6%	9%	12%	15%	18%	21%
0%	12	15	21				
2%	11	13	16	24			
4%	10	11	14	17			
6%	9	10	12	14	19		
8%	9	10	11	13	15	22	
10%	8	9	10	11	13	17	26
12%	8	9	9	11	12	14	18
14%	8	8	9	10	11	13	15

TABLE 3 If you plan to withdraw the inflation-adjusted equivalent of 15% of your original invested capital, the numbers will be

Inflation	Total return on balance →						
	3%	6%	9%	12%	15%	18%	21%
0%	8	9	10	12	15		
2%	7	8	9	10	12	17	
4%	7	8	8	9	11	13	19
6%	7	7	8	9	10	11	14
8%	6	7	7	8	9	10	12
10%	6	7	7	8	8	9	10
12%	6	6	7	7	8	8	9
14%	6	6	6	7	7	8	9

EXAMPLE:
You have an asset base of $200,000.

You would like to withdraw $20,000 a year or 10% of the $200,000.

Your assets are earning 9% and you expect inflation to average 6% over the coming years.

Use Table 2 (10% Withdrawal Rate).

You will be able to withdraw $20,000 and the inflation-adjusted equivalent every year for 12 years before running out of capital.

EXAMPLE:
You have an asset base of $200,000.

You want to know how much you can withdraw each year for the next 30 years and never run out.

Your assets are earning 15% and you expect inflation to average 8%

a) If you withdraw 5% ($10,000) your capital will last over 30 years.

b) If you withdraw 10% or $20,000, you will run out in 15 years.

Whether you do it yourself or call in the experts, there is some key financial information you must collect and organize before any plan can be developed. A financial plan is comprehensive. It looks at your entire financial picture in order to create an integrated whole. Planning and a plan are related but not the same.

Here are the building blocks of a solid workable financial plan and what information will be needed in order to develop one. After each are listed the forms in **MONEY MINDER** that help you prepare for a plan.

| Net Worth | Where are you today? What assets do you have already and how are they distributed? |

NET WORTH AT A GLANCE p. 29
NET WORTH IN DETAIL p. 31

| Cash Flow | What is your current and projected income from all sources and how are you spending it? How much could be diverted to savings/investing? |

MONEY IN, MONEY OUT, pp. 21, 23
NOW WHAT? p. 25

| Protection | Are you adequately protected personally and against major losses to your asset base? |

INSURANCE p. 67

| Tax Liability | What are you paying now? Could better planning reduce your taxes? |

TAXES p. 69
TAX FORMS CHECKLIST p. 71

| Asset Allocation | How are your assets distributed? Should they be repositioned? |

ASSET ALLOCATION p. 75
NET WORTH pp. 29, 31

| Personal Needs/Goals | What kind of a person are you? What special needs do you have? What goals? What is your tolerance for risk? How involved do you want to be? |

WHERE AND HOW p. 15
GOALS p. 17
MANAGING YOURSELF p. 5

| Retirement | What Social Security benefits can you anticipate? Pension? IRAs and other deferred sources of income? |

SOCIAL SECURITY p. 59
RETIREMENT OUT p. 57

Plans are like road maps. A lot stays the same, but some things change so be prepared to refine your plan over time. With your **MONEY MINDER** forms up-to-date, you'll always have the critical information ready to go.

Most published forms are designed for the average person, but who's average? The forms that will work best for you are the ones you design or adapt for yourself.

MONEY MINDER covers a wide variety of situations, but some of you will have a special need or you might want to try your own hand.

Here are the major ingredients for designing your own.
The basics are:
- ☐ Space for a heading
- ☐ Space to indicate the preparation date, year, owner as needed
- ☐ Wide lines
- ☐ A place at the bottom for notes

On p. 117 is a lined format sized to fit an 8½ × 11 page with room at the top and bottom.
- ☐ Use it to record or track anything of personal or financial importance: an insurance claim, application for Social Security benefits, interviewing and selecting a financial advisor, preparing for a vacation.

On p. 118 is a grid sized like the **MONEY MINDER** forms with wide enough spaces and lines to be comfortable to use.
- ☐ Use it to compare/evaluate alternatives or when you want more columns than on a regular page (See Asset Allocation p. 97). Compare investments, medical insurance plans, tax preparation services, new cars.

On p. 119 is a graph format. For some people it is fun, sometimes, to dispense with the numbers and create a picture of what's going on. There is some truth in the saying a picture is worth a thousand words.
- ☐ Use it to picture how your savings/investments are growing, how your assets are shifting, what proportion you are saving/investing.

On p. 120 are some examples that might inspire you. You will increase the impact of all of these creations dramatically by adding color. Financial information does not have to be drab!

Notes _____

Tracking Annuity ► WORKSHEET

Date	Amount	gaur. Interest
1978	10,170	7.65
1979	10,921	8.02
1980	11,797	8.75
1981	12,892	9.00
1982	13,984	9.00
1983	15,243	8.55

2/88   Comparing ► Heath Insurance

	Cost (monthly)	Coverage	Convenience	Choice of Doctors	Reputation	Application Process	Hospital
Statewide	141	Excell.	8 mi.	some	good	very friendly	15 yrs. old
City HMO	162	good	4 mi.	Pick your own	Excell.	O.K.	Less than 5 yrs.
Quality Care	154	fair	10 mi.	some	good	O.K.	new wing

Notes _____

170—									
160—									
150—									
140—									
130—									
120—									
110—									
100—									
90—									
80—									
70—									
60—									
50—									
40—									
30—									
20—									
10,000									

Self Spouse Home Rental Stocks Bonds Funds Ltd Cash Retire.
Insurance Real Estate Securities Part Equip. ment

Every field has its special vocabulary. here are a few words and terms used in the world of money management. It is sometimes important to understand and use them carefully in communicating with banks, accountants, the IRS, and financials advisers. Some of these words are used differently by different people. They might not mean what you mean. I have tried to provide the basic meaning of each word, rather than all its technical ramifications and exceptions.

Basis—Often called **cost basis** or **price basis**, the original cost of an investment *plus* additions, reinvestments, or out-of-pocket expenses that you report to the IRS at the

time you sell in order to establish capital gains or losses. These additions to the original cost increase the basis so they lower the profit tax you would pay on gains and increase the losses you can claim on a capital loss.

Capital gain—Any increase in the value of an asset. Under current law, capital gain is taxed as regular income.

Short-term capital gain—Profits from an investment that are taxed as ordinary income, currently defined by the federal government as less than one year.
Long-term capital gain—Profits from an investment that have been held one year or more and are taxed at a more favorable rate. Favorable treatment is being phased out gradually under provisions of the Tax Reform Act of 1986, but many people are predicting it will be reinstated in some form within next five years.

Capitalize—To treat an expenditure as an addition to assets, rather than an expense. This has tax consequences. If you capitalize a new carpet for an apartment owned as a rental property, you must *depreciate* (deduct) its value over a period of years on your tax returns. If you are able treat it as a maintenance replacement it can be *expensed*— fully deducted in the year you paid for it.

Equity—1.) Fairness as in an equitable decision. 2.) Ownership—the percentage or dollars representing your share of your home, the shareholders' interest in a corporation, or the excess of assets over debits in a margin brokerage account. Stocks are frequently referred to as equities.

Ex-dividends—Literally, without dividend. A condition created by the time between the announcement of a dividend and its actual payment to owners. If you purchase a stock that has gone ex-dividend, the seller gets the dividend. The company specifies a record date to indicate the last day on which the seller is entitled to the dividend. The stock exchanges usually announce the dividend three days before the record date.

Face value or par value—The value stated on the face of a note, bond, mortgage, or insurance policy. For bonds, the interest rate quoted is based on this amount even though you can buy the bond at a **discount** (below face value) or **premium** (above) and be getting a higher or lower current yield in relation to your actual cost. In insurance, face value represents the death benefit you will receive (minus any loans outstanding against the policy) and the **cash value** (if any) is the amount you can borrow against, using the policy as collateral.

Property—There are different ways to own (have title to) property (any asset). Each involve issues of ownership, control, inheritance, and taxes. Following are the most common.

Separate—Sometimes called **individual property.** Property fully owned by one person.

Joint tenancy—Property owned by two or more people. Any of the joint owners can sell, transfer, withdraw, use the entire property without the approval/signature of any other owner. Upon the death of one or more owners title passes immediately to the survivors. There are no tax consequences.

Tenancy in common—Property owned and controlled by two or more each with a specified share usually expressed as a proportion such as one half or one third. Signatures of all owners are required for any transactions. Upon the death of one or more owners their share passes to their estate and is taxed accordingly. The other owner(s) retain their proportionate shares and all accompanying rights.

Community property—Property owned equally (50% each) by a husband and wife. Like joint tenancy, can be controlled or used by either party except that a spouse operating a community property business can manage it exclusively. Upon death, the surviving spouse retains ownership of one half and the other half becomes part of the the estate of deceased. All property left to a surviving spouse is transferred tax free. The IRS and some community property states, such as California, step up the cost basis and revalue *all* community property left to the surviving spouse as of the date of death not just the deceased's share. This can have substantial tax consequences for assets that have appreciated and be an important consideration in estate planning.

Power of attorney—A document authorizing another person to act in your behalf signing legal papers or transferring funds. Can be *limited*, as within a discretionary account with a brokerage firm or *full*, allowing transfer between accounts, banks, etc. . Until recently a power of attorney terminated automatically when someone became infirm or died. Today many states recognize a *durable power of attorney* that specifically authorizes whoever you appoint to act in your behalf if you are incapacitated. This is well worth considering if you are elderly, have no relatives nearby, or are considering a serious medical procedure. Look for the forms in a good stationery store.

Recapture—To sell an asset and in certain circumstances have to take back or figure into your final profit/loss the depreciation taken previously. As an investor what this means is what the government gives, it takes back—sometimes.

Return—Often used as the yield or income from an investment—sometimes includes appreciation and tax benefits. Be sure to verify how the speaker is using the word. There is no common agreement.

Rate of return—Income/results achieved by an investment on an annualized basis expressed as a percent.

Total return—The most complete measure of an investment. Includes income, appreciation, and tax benefits (amount saved in actual taxes) over the life of the investment or whatever period you are measuring.

Internal rate of return—A measure of the results of an investment, taking into account the lost economic opportunity cost of the dollars invested. There is no common agreement how it is figured. It is useful in comparing investments only if the same formula is applied to all investments being evaluated.

Rollover (IRA)—1.) Any movement of IRA accounts where funds are sent to you. They must be reinvested within 60 days and *only one rollover is allowed in any 12-month period per IRA account.* (You can have more than one account.) 2.) Any tax-free lump sum distribution of more than 50% of a qualified plan to another qualified plan or IRA.

Settlement date (for purchases and sales)—Date when funds are due.

Short-term/long-term losses—Same basic principles apply. Losses up to $3,000 are fully deductible in the year they occur. Currently, losses beyond $3,000 can be carried forward and deducted in future years.

Tax bracket (or marginal tax rate)—The percent you would have to pay in taxes on the next dollar of taxable income. This is important because we have a graduated income tax. Financial advisers use this measure frequently in estimating the benefits of different investments. That is, you can make money directly from an investment or in taxes saved. Tax brackets can be inferred from the tax rate schedules in your income tax booklet but do not appear on the tax tables. You can also get them from your tax preparer or through reference books or brokers.

Tax credit—A dollar for dollar reduction in taxes due.

Tax liability—The *amount* you owe the government at any point in time. Your tax liability at tax time—whether you owe a lot or get a refund—is much less important than your total tax liability for the year and how that relates to your income.

Trade date (for stock/bond purchases and sales)—The date when transaction is made. For tax purposes, always use the trade date.

Write-off—A deduction from income made in determining taxable income *before* estimating your taxes.

Yield—Income or cash flow. It can be dividends or interest. Usually is expressed on an annualized percent. Because of compounding the yield might be higher than the expressed rate of return. (For example: A C. D. has a quoted rate of return of 10% but because of compounding of interest, actually yields 10.5%.)